GUIDE TO ACADEMIC AND SCIENTIFIC PUBLICATION

How To Get Your Writing Published in Scholarly Journals

Linda Olson

D.Phil., English and Related Literature

D1734212

Published by

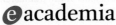 academia

Letchworth Garden City, 2014

First edition, 2014.

Copyright © Published by eacademia, 2014

Printed for eacademia in Dubai by Oriental Press.

ISBN 978-0-9929588-0-0 Paperback

ACKNOWLEDGEMENTS

I would like to thank all the scholars (students, professors and fellow academics) whose writing I've marked, edited and proofread over the years. Without them and their work, I could never have gained the knowledge and experience required to write this *Guide*. I am also grateful to René and Judith for their helpful comments while the *Guide* was in progress.

Linda Olson

ABOUT THIS GUIDE

Written by an academic author, editor and proofreader, this *Guide to Academic and Scientific Publication* provides practical advice on planning, preparing and submitting articles for publication in scholarly journals. Whether you're looking for information on designing an academic or scientific article, constructing a scholarly argument, targeting the right journal, following journal guidelines with precision, providing accurate and complete references, writing elegant scholarly English, communicating with journal editors or revising your paper in light of that communication, you'll find guidance, tips and examples in this manual. Focussing on sound scholarly practices as well as the expectations and requirements of academic and scientific journals, this *Guide* is suitable for use in a wide variety of disciplines, including the Social, Physical and Biological Sciences, the Humanities, Medicine, Engineering, Mathematics, Economics, Law and Management.

Please note that this *Guide to Academic and Scientific Publication* also includes a number of Proof-Reading-Service.com (PRS) Tips. These offer advice on a variety of practical matters and are enclosed in coloured text boxes that make them easy to locate.

TABLE OF CONTENTS

PART I:
WHAT TO PUBLISH AND WHERE TO PUBLISH IT

Chapter 1: **Essential Ingredients for a Successful Academic or Scientific Article** 1

    1.1 Research: Methods, Practices and Sources 2

    1.2 Evidence: Discoveries, Results and Data 4

    1.3 Argument: What Does It Mean and Why Is It Important? 6

    1.4 Minimum Publishable Units 9

Chapter 2: **Targeting an Academic or Scientific Journal: The Right Paper in the Right Place** 11

    2.1 Choosing the Journal that Fits and Benefits Your Work 11

        • 2.1.1 Range and Specialisation: Is It the Right Fit? 11

        • 2.1.2 Journal Importance, Citation Reports and Impact Factor: Will It Have the Right Effect? 13

    2.2 Shaping Your Work To Fit the Journal 15

PART II:
PREPARING, PRESENTING AND POLISHING YOUR WORK

Chapter 3: **Deciphering Journal Guidelines and Designing an Effective Presentation** 19

    3.1 Titles, Headings and Subheadings: Not Just Fancy Words 21

    3.2 Paragraphs and Lists: Effective Presentation and Transition 26

        • 3.2.1 Structured and Fully Developed Paragraphs 26

        • 3.2.2 Using Lists Effectively 28

TABLE OF CONTENTS

Chapter 4: **Journal Guidelines and Formal Scholarly English** **30**

4.1 British versus American English 30

4.2 Understanding Abbreviations 31

4.3 Punctuating Appropriately 35

4.4 Finding Your Scholarly Voice 38

• 4.4.1 Vocabulary: Formality, Precision and Variety 39

• 4.4.2 English Verbs: Tensing Up and Splitting Hairs 42

• 4.4.3 Using Pronouns Professionally and Clearly 47

Chapter 5: **Presenting Data and Sources Accurately and Effectively** **52**

5.1 Tables, Figures and Other Research Data: Guidelines and Good Practice 52

5.2 Last but Not Least: References, Citations and Quotations 57

• 5.2.1 In-Text Citations and Quotations: Where and How To Acknowledge Sources 59

• 5.2.2 Footnotes and Endnotes: Do You Need Them? 67

• 5.2.3 Reference Lists and Bibliographies: Niggling Details 69

5.3 Automatic Formatting: To Use or Not To Use 74

TABLE OF CONTENTS

PART III:
COMMUNICATING WITH JOURNAL EDITORS: SUBMISSION, ACCEPTANCE, REVISION AND REJECTION

Chapter 6: **First Things First: Earning the Interest and Respect of an Academic or Scientific Editor** .. **78**

6.1 Covering Letters: First Impressions 79

6.2 Titles, Abstracts and Keywords: Sound Connections 81

• 6.2.1 The Very Beginning: The Title 82

• 6.2.2 Summing It All Up: The Abstract 84

• 6.2.3 Searching for the Right Terms: The Keywords 87

6.3 Ready and Willing: Submission Procedures 88

Chapter 7: **After Submission: Acceptance, Rejection and Revision** **92**

7.1 'Just What We're Looking For': The Successful Publishing Relationship 92

7.2 When 'No' Means No: Professional Departures and New Beginnings 94

7.3 'We're Interested but...': The Revision Process ... 96

• 7.3.1 Formatting, Structure and Referencing Style 97

• 7.3.2 Language and Clarity 98

• 7.3.3 Content: Methods, Data and Argument... 100

APPENDIX

Sample Responses to Letters from Academic and Scientific Editors 105

Letter A.1: Earning or Confirming Serious Reconsideration or Conditional Acceptance 106

Letter A.2: Resubmitting a Paper after Necessary Revisions Have Been Made 108

Part I:
What To Publish and Where To Publish It

CHAPTER 1
Essential Ingredients for a Successful Academic or Scientific Article

Preparing an article for publication in an academic or scientific journal can feel rather like balancing on a tightrope – a tightrope intricately woven of many finely crafted strands. The strands must be sound and enduring, much like the material that goes into the making of a good paper: the research, methods, theories, experiments, analyses and conclusions that are woven together into an academic or scientific article. The tightrope itself is rather like the argument of the paper. Vulnerable spots created by weak materials or poor weaving can bring down both the rope and the rope walker, much as weak evidence and a poorly constructed argument can fail to convince (or even interest) a reader and ultimately produce an effect very different from what the author had anticipated. Guiding readers successfully along the intellectual paths and scientific discoveries that have proven so fascinating and eminently publishable is the goal of every scholarly writer, and no author wants the attention of the reader to slip away. No academic or scientific writer wants to jeopardise his or her professional reputation either, and balancing on that tightrope is an apt analogy for the challenges of producing truly valuable scholarly work at the rapid pace demanded by the publish-or-perish environment of a modern digital world.

There is, of course, no one foolproof method for producing an excellent article, and each paper involves a number of decisions that only the author can make about the content, structure and presentation necessary to report unique research in ways that are acceptable and effective within a given field or discipline. There are, however, a number of concerns that every academic or scientific writer should consider carefully while planning and writing a manuscript for publication, and there are approaches and techniques that tend to be far more successful than others. These concerns, approaches and techniques are the matters on which this *Guide to Academic and Scientific Publication* focuses.

1.1   Research: Methods, Practices and Sources

Whether the research you're planning to publish is based upon a single text or experiment or is only a small part of a much larger project, you will need to decide exactly what to include and what to exclude while planning and drafting your paper. Certainly this decision will be based on the word limits set by the journal (or journals) in which you're hoping to publish your work, and some authors may wish to choose a journal at this point (see Chapter 2 below) and use its guidelines to help determine the content, structure and layout of their writing. While it's certainly a good idea to take a careful look at not just journal guidelines but articles already published in the journals you may be considering as you're designing your paper, it's usually best to begin by focussing on your research. Choosing the methods, practices and sources that will best test or support your theories is essential, and so, too, is explaining them and the reasons why they are appropriate for your research as clearly as possible to your readers.

Perhaps your study began with a wide review of literature on your research topic or an extensive search through national registers of demographic information. Maybe you used trials, experiments, tests, controls, surveys, group discussions, interviews or direct observation in gathering your data. Perhaps you found your sources online or in a medieval manuscript library or maybe you used only the spoken words of people encountered randomly on the street. Whatever the case may be, the key is to keep careful and exact records of exactly what you've done and be prepared to explain your approaches precisely and in enough detail that your readers will clearly understand your procedures. Often a lack of clear explanation about methodology results from the simple fact that researchers become so familiar with and immersed in their own research that the basics seem too obvious to require explanation. However, even readers familiar with the academic or scientific territory traversed in your scholarly paper need to be informed about your approaches and practices to understand the significance of your work: if your methodology doesn't come across as clear and valid, neither will your results or any argument you base upon them.

A clear explanation of your methodology need not take up a large part of your paper – usually a few carefully worded sentences will do the trick; sometimes a few paragraphs are required – but it achieves a great deal. It provides you with the opportunity not only to inform your reader about exactly what your research is and how you do it, but also to substantiate and justify your work: as you outline your reasons for choosing the approaches and sources you used, you can also explain to your readers why they are indeed the most penetrating and reliable approaches available to produce effective and meaningful results in your field of study. In addition, you can clarify exactly what is innovative or derivative about your work and why, and although this generally comes far later in the paper than descriptions of methodology, you can also outline the limitations of your study. Anticipating potential criticisms of your methodology and taking special care when explaining any aspects that may seem weak or ineffective to your readers are often extremely helpful when trying to describe exactly what is unique and valuable about your work.

In many ways deciding upon and explaining your methods, practices and sources is simply a matter of positioning yourself within your field of study or specialisation and justifying your own perspective as an informed and thoughtful one. I once had a creative writing teacher who insisted that perspective was the most important aspect of fiction – without an understanding of where he or she is writing from, he argued, no author can even begin – and this is equally true of scholarly writing, though in somewhat different ways. Establishing your perspective is an essential part of developing your voice as a writer, and when you're writing academic or scientific prose, that voice needs to be professional and authoritative (see Section 4.4 below). Explaining how sound the methodology you've developed or adopted is makes for a great start, but scholarly authority must ultimately be supported by solid and reliable evidence if your article is to be a success.

1.2   Evidence: Discoveries, Results and Data

The evidence presented in a scholarly paper – the discoveries, results and data that stem from the research – is in many ways the heart of any article. Were the evidence discovered through the approaches you adopted not convincing or interesting or original or useful, there would be little point in writing a paper to share that evidence and your means of obtaining it with the scholarly community. Describing even the most wonderful and promising of studies is not enough on its own: the researcher needs to decide exactly what he or she has learned, why and what aspects of that new knowledge are significant, and then make both that knowledge and its importance clear for readers of the article. By writing at all, the academic or scientific author assumes that the information he or she has to share will be new and of both immediate and abiding interest to others working in the same field, and often beyond it, and that this information will therefore influence the nature and direction of future research in the area. In order to achieve such lofty goals, the evidence must be both significant and sound, and it must also be presented to readers in ways that make clear exactly what has and has not been shown as well as what those results might mean.

It is the job of each author to make sure that his or her evidence, just like his or her methodology, meets the standards of acceptability and validity within the relevant field of study. These standards will differ considerably between disciplines, of course, but clarity is central to presenting evidence effectively no matter what the topic may be. This can be challenging: presenting data in ways that are both precise and interesting as well as grammatically correct and, if at all possible, eloquent is no easy task, as anyone who has written 'more than' or 'compared with' or 'in relation to' for the fourth or fifth time in a paragraph is well aware. There is an enormous temptation to cut corners by using, for instance, pronouns instead of precise nouns and words such as 'former' and 'latter' instead of repeating full descriptions of data in order to avoid repetition in the main text. Such efforts at condensation can be successful and they can certainly result in unencumbered language if they are very carefully worded, but when it comes to reporting results, they are rarely as effective as clear, simply structured sentences that outline with exact nouns and verbs precisely what has been discovered or determined (on the use of pronouns and precise language, see Sections 4.4.1 & 4.4.3).

If you are a virtuoso of scholarly English prose, by all means flaunt your style when reporting the results and discoveries of your research: a clear and eloquently written Results section is a rare and admirable accomplishment in any academic or scientific paper and should definitely be a goal for those who wish to make a career of writing scholarly prose. Do remember, however, when planning how you will present evidence in your paper that the skill needed to achieve this sort of eloquence is most often acquired through years of practice and experience, and the first goal of any researcher attempting to share his or her results is clear communication. A long, beautifully constructed sentence with clever turns of phrases and five parenthetical clauses may roll pleasingly off the tongue (or not), but it may also confuse readers who simply aren't as familiar with your results as you are, particularly if precise, detailed description is compromised for the sake of style. So three shorter sentences, for instance, no matter how simply structured or seemingly dull, may prove far more successful for factually laying out the exact nature of your evidence and results in a way that can be readily understood by your readers. That evidence is usually complicated enough on its own, so trying to keep the ways in which you report it as simple as possible can be most beneficial for both your paper and your readers.

Often tables, graphs and illustrations can be immensely helpful in presenting complex evidence clearly and concisely in as little space as possible, so it's a good idea to decide before drafting your paper exactly what information might work well in tables and figures, and what information will not. Study designs, numerical data, the details of control and intervention groups, and any other material that can be assessed and compared at a glance are particularly effective in tables, and figures can provide not just illustrations of devices and details but also charts, plots and graphs that present evidence in striking visual forms. Tables and figures are only as useful as they are well designed, however, so clarity and accuracy is required in all the elements of tables and figures: columns, rows, charts and graphs should be laid out as tidily as possible to relate and separate information in a manner that avoids confusion. Any abbreviations used in a table or figure should be defined or explained in the table or figure itself because each table or figure should be comprehensible on its own, without the reader having to refer back to the text. The title of a table or the caption for a figure should also be explanatory: that is, it should describe exactly what the table or figure shows, including brief clarifications of any information about categories, values, comparisons and so on that are outlined in more detail in the paper itself. So if you're hoping to use tables and figures, keep these basic requirements in mind as you work on your designs and only plan on using tables and figures if you are fairly certain they will successfully communicate to your readers evidence central to your study (for more information on tables and figures, see Section 5.1 below).

1.3   Argument: What Does It Mean and Why Is It Important?

Although it seems that argument sometimes plays second fiddle to other aspects of scholarly prose, a carefully constructed argument is as essential to a good academic or scientific article as methodology and evidence – indeed, the argument or thesis of a scholarly paper encompasses all other aspects of a paper and also allows the author to share thoughts as original and engaging as the research and results from which the argument has grown. Although the argument of any given paper can only be finally determined after the research has been done and the evidence collected, it generally begins as the seed of that research, develops slowly as the work progresses and tends to influence the questions that are asked as well as the ways in which they are answered. What your study and its results mean and why that meaning is important should be considered as central as methodology and results when planning a successful paper. If you think your research worth writing about, then presumably you have a number of thoughts about it that are also worth sharing, and wherever these thoughts began or however they've grown, for the purposes of an academic or scientific article they need to be developed into a sustained, logical argument that both focuses closely on the particular research and provides a larger intellectual or scientific context in which to consider it.

Most scholars will have encountered the basics of academic and scientific argumentation very early on in their education, and most journals will require sections that highlight the argument of a paper, so it may seem redundant to repeat those basics here. However, it can at times be notoriously tricky to incorporate these basics when reporting the complexities of academic or scientific research, so recalling them and their purposes can be helpful. In brief, a basic scholarly argument involves introducing the problem or topic by providing background, context, current situation, previous literature and experiments, and so on. You need not review every publication on the topic or consider every current concern – that would be appropriate for a book or thesis; an article is more focussed – but you should say enough to allow your reader to understand your study and its importance, and to show that you are well aware of all the sources and approaches with which you should be familiar to conduct the study successfully. Next, you should explain how you've approached the problem by describing and justifying your methodology (as discussed in Section 1.1 above), and then report the evidence you've discovered through that methodology (as discussed in Section 1.2 above).

The more creative part of the argument usually comes in the discussion of that evidence and the conclusions you draw from it: here, you can basically do what you will with your research so long as you maintain logical argumentation, keep your conclusions reasonable in relation to your methods and results, and, as always, carefully explain your thinking, especially where it may differ significantly from previous scholarship in the area, because what may seem obvious to you, steeped in your own research as you are, may not seem obvious at all to your readers. This process is far more easily described than done, of course, and there is a fine line between underwriting and overwriting when working to explain one's thought processes – another example of how academic and scientific authors must balance on that textual tightrope – but there are a number of simple questions that can be asked to facilitate effective argumentation, such as:

- Have I explained my thinking clearly and thoroughly enough for readers to understand?
- Is the terminology I'm using effective and precise for expressing my thoughts?
- Have I valued my research and its implications fairly?
- Does the evidence I report support my conclusions?
- Have I considered all the conclusions that might follow from the evidence?
- Do I make the limitations of the study clear?
- If I use conjecture or generalisation, have I qualified it adequately for the reader?

The aim of these and many other questions that might be asked about a scholarly argument is to achieve a high quality of both thought and communication. If you haven't accurately assessed your work, reflected at length upon its implications and come to valid conclusions, then you will find it extremely difficult to devise a cogent and valuable argument about that work and communicate it to your readers. Even when a sound argument has been formed in the mind, it can be extremely difficult to present it effectively in prose: juggling the ongoing progress of an argument with citations from earlier studies and the usually complicated results of your own work is never easy, especially when the word limitations set by most journals come into play. In my experience, the best policy is to plan on writing whatever is needed to explain everything you want to say thoroughly, and then edit and, if need be, shorten it after it's been drafted. Editing is, after all, a necessary and oft-repeated aspect of any accomplished piece of writing, and shortening your paper is best done once you have a clear idea of where you'll be submitting it and the requirements regarding structure and length with which you'll be working.

Ideally, you'll also be able to benefit from the criticism of a colleague in your field of study who is willing to read your work and offer advice. Constructive criticism is useful no matter how frequently an author has produced and successfully published writing in the past, but if you're a graduate student just beginning to publish your work, it's absolutely crucial. Much can be learned by reading published articles, and every scientist or academic aims to achieve the highest scholarly standards in his or her writing, but intentions and results – what we plan to do opposed to what our writing actually does – can, as any researcher knows, be very different things at times, and there is no substitute for having someone who understands exactly what you're writing about and knows exactly what's expected in your field read and comment on your work. Your academic supervisor or advisor is the ideal person to provide guidance as you work at achieving your first publication, but any senior scholar (ideally one who has successfully published) in your area will suffice, and fellow students can be very helpful readers as well.

1.4   Minimum Publishable Units

There is incredible pressure on modern academics and scientists to publish frequently in order to receive promotions, grants and salary increases, so there is also an enormous temptation to cut projects, studies and articles up into smaller units in order to squeeze more publications out of the same amount of work. There are certain types of paper which might, in comparison with a full research article, be considered partial studies: a study protocol in which a project is simply described, for instance, and a literature review which aims to outline what has been published on a topic to date. For most academic and scientific papers, however, and certainly for the kind of original research paper that tends to establish a scholar as an authority, providing a minimum publishable unit is required.

By a minimum publishable unit I mean a complete study – one that contains and explains the three elements (original research, significant results and a meaningful argument) discussed in this Chapter. A short paper can represent a minimum publishable unit for a brief study if all of these elements are present, but a complete study divided into shorter sections to achieve more publications does not necessarily result in a number of publishable research papers, and repeating material in different studies to shore up their deficiencies is not the answer either. These approaches tend to produce papers that stand a better chance of being rejected than accepted by reputable journals, and even if they are accepted, they will almost certainly be accepted in journals that are less than top tier. So while it is tempting to stretch your research out over as many articles as possible, your time will be much better spent (and your professional reputation much better served) by preparing a complete and accomplished piece of academic or scientific writing that will be appropriate for publication as original research in a highly respected journal that suits your work perfectly (on which, see Chapter 2 below).

PRS Tip:
Although this Guide focuses on the preparation of academic and scientific articles for journal publication, the PRS team is happy to proofread a wide variety of documents in English. We specialise in all kinds of scholarly texts, including conference papers, books, dissertations and theses as well as articles, but we're also delighted to proofread letters, grant proposals and teaching materials. Whatever sort of academic or scientific text you're busy composing, if you'd appreciate a second set of careful, professional eyes to help perfect your writing, do send your document our way.

CHAPTER 2
Targeting an Academic or Scientific Journal: The Right Paper in the Right Place

With the basic design of your article in mind, your tables and figures planned (if not yet actually constructed) and perhaps your paper drafted as well, you will need to choose a journal that is appropriate for your work before making final decisions about structure and presentation. Each journal will provide different guidelines or instructions for authors to follow, some of them very detailed and specific, others much less so, allowing authors a great deal more flexibility in terms of how they prepare their writing. Occasionally, such guidelines will need to be considered when choosing a journal: if you simply cannot describe the nature of your study, report your results and construct your argument effectively in less than 8,000 words and seven tables, a journal that calls for papers no longer than 4,000 words with no more than two tables simply will not do for that paper. However, decisions about where to submit your work are generally determined not by such practical details, but by considering the overall nature of both your work and the journal in which you'd like to see that work published.

2.1 Choosing the Journal that Fits and Benefits Your Work

2.1.1 Range and Specialisation: Is It the Right Fit?

It may seem painfully obvious to say that when you plan to submit an academic or scientific article for publication you need to select a journal with great care, but the fact is that the decision-making process is too often not given enough time and attention. Certainly most authors do try to submit medical papers to medical journals, literary papers to literary journals and geological papers to geological journals, but there should be far more to the decision than that. One literary journal, for example, may consider a wide range of world literature, encompassing fiction and nonfiction, prose and poetry in a variety of languages, while another will focus very closely on one genre in one language from a single period (Middle English poetry, for instance), and still another might only publish work on a particular author (William Shakespeare comes to mind as an author with more than one dedicated journal). Some journals pride themselves on being extremely traditional, while others consider themselves unorthodox and avant-garde in terms of what they publish, and some limit their articles to particular themes or approaches, so while one might welcome a close textual analysis of an English meditation on suicide, another is looking for a theoretical study of French love poetry from a feminist or deconstructionist perspective. Sending a paper on one of these topics to a journal editor who would be pleased to publish the other will never lead to publishing success.

The key, then, to choosing the right journal is to learn as much as possible about the range and specialisation of the journals under consideration. Check the 'About us' pages on their web sites to find out what their goals and mission statements are; scan archived issues to detect prevalent themes and topic areas; read papers they've already published, especially any articles that sound as though they deal with the same topic as yours or use similar methodology. Use the sources that serve as the inspiration for your own work as a guide: if a number of them are published in the same journal, that's an excellent journal to explore. If your academic supervisor is helping you with critical advice on your paper, use a discussion of his or her feedback as an opportunity to ask which journal he or she thinks might be a good fit for your work. If you have colleagues publishing work much like your own, find out where they're publishing and if they might have any helpful advice. If you've published your work in a journal before, your chances of being published by the same journal are good – certainly the editor will attend carefully to your new paper – but that alone is not reason enough to send your work to that journal. Only if your new article suits the journal's publishing agenda as well as the one already published in it did (or if you've been lucky enough to receive an open invitation to submit future work) should you submit to the same journal. As much care should be taken over a good publishing relationship as over a good academic or scientific paper, and a good publishing relationship is fostered by sending top quality work that fits.

It can sometimes be helpful to contact a journal before deciding to submit your paper. Not all journals will welcome such queries, however, so if the guidelines suggest that this is not wanted – that is, that only full submissions are requested – don't pursue this approach. If, on the other hand, the journal invites queries in advance of submission or it seems that a query letter might be an effective means of first contact with a journal that simply doesn't have the space to include all the publishable papers it receives, it can be useful to send a message outlining the point of your study and including a summary of your paper (an early draft of the abstract would serve this purpose well, but be sure to polish and perfect it before sending it along: see Section 6.2.2). If you learn from your query that the topic or methodology of your paper would make it a low priority for the journal, it doesn't mean that you should abandon your efforts to publish your paper in that journal if that is your preference, but you will have a better understanding of the challenges you face and can then decide whether you should continue your efforts to publish in that journal or spend your time seeking an appropriate journal with which you stand a better chance of success.

2.1.2 Journal Importance, Citation Reports and Impact Factor: Will It Have the Right Effect?

Along with range and specialisation, the importance of a journal should be considered as you're deciding where to submit your work. In all disciplines, word of mouth and experience as a reader is your first guide to the importance or authority of an academic or scientific journal. Every field of study has a few journals that rise above the rest – the sort of journals in which the most significant and innovative work by leading academics or scientists in the field is published. Succeeding at having work published in such a journal can earn scholarly respect, make a professional reputation and go a long way toward establishing a healthy career. These journals are well known to everyone associated with a discipline and widely read, so it is easy enough to identify them and discover the kind of work they publish. It is more difficult, however, to decide whether your work is appropriate for such a journal, if for no other reason than because such a judgement involves accurate self-assessment, so the advice of colleagues and mentors recruited as critical readers will be particularly helpful for this reason as well. If you undervalue your work by not submitting to such journals, you'll never be published in them, but if you overvalue your work by submitting it when it's not appropriate, your work will almost certainly be rejected, so again, you need to submit your work to one of these highly respected journals only if it fits the journal's publishing agenda in both content and significance, not simply because you'd really like to be published in it.

Just because any given piece of work isn't appropriate for such top-tier journals doesn't mean that it shouldn't be published, however, and it can be much more practical, especially as you're working to find your authorial voice early in your career, to choose an appropriate, reputable journal for whose pages there isn't quite as much competition. It's always best to choose a refereed or peer-reviewed journal because this means that the research articles published by that journal have been evaluated by scholars and researchers who specialise in the subject area. This process tends to eliminate articles with flaws in content, and journals that use it tend to earn academic and scientific respect and influence. *Ulrich's Periodical Directory*, online access to which can be gained through most university libraries, can be used to determine if a journal is peer-reviewed, and Journal Citation Reports, also available through most university libraries, provides a way of evaluating the research influence and impact of more than 10,000 science and social sciences journals. In the second of these publications, citations of research articles are recorded and the number of times the articles published by each journal have been cited over the course of a year is determined to construct an inclusive journal citation network. Citations of the articles published by a journal are averaged to provide an impact factor for the journal over either a two-year or five-year period, as well as an immediacy index, which indicates the number of times articles published by the journal in a given year have been cited in that same year.

Citation reports and impact factors can be extremely helpful when choosing an influential and respected journal that will effectively make your work accessible to a large number of the readers for whom you're writing, but they should be used with caution. Citation rates in the first years after publication vary from discipline to discipline and even within a discipline one article can be cited a hundred times more often than the next article, thereby greatly improving the impact factor of a journal that nonetheless tends to publish articles that are rarely cited. There are also a number of ways in which journals can deliberately skew the citation data: by including, for instance, a smaller number of articles that are unlikely to be cited, no matter how publishable and valuable they may be, and a larger number of review articles which tend to be cited more often than research reports. Some journals even use a policy of coercive citation, a practice in which a journal editor forces an author to add spurious citations of articles published by the journal and thus increase the journal's impact factor before agreeing to publish his or her paper. Such unethical practices suggest that competition for top ratings among academic and scientific journals is as fierce as that for publication in them among academic authors, but the best way in which journals can truly improve their ratings and academics and scientists can have a significant impact through their writing is by maintaining a close focus on scholarship that is as honest as it is accomplished.

2.2   Shaping Your Work To Fit the Journal

Producing honest and accomplished scholarship does not mean that you can't stack the deck in your favour, however, when submitting your writing to the journal you've chosen. In fact, you should use everything you can learn about the journal to your advantage, and one of the classic ways of making your paper a good fit for a journal is to read and cite articles already published in that journal. If you've done your research by reading articles published in the journal that are similar to your own in order to choose the journal in the first place, this will prove easy and a natural progression of your scholarship that really does make your work compatible with other papers in the journal.

The way in which you introduce your work to the journal's editor is vital as well. You need to understand what the journal is looking for and then explain to the editor exactly why your paper fits the bill. This does not mean compromising your methodology, evidence or argument, but the same paper can look very different when addressed to different audiences. Your covering letter is usually (not always) the first document the journal's editor will read, and much can be accomplished in a couple of paragraphs. Take the opportunity to describe your paper in ways that appeal to the journal's concerns: if you've come to innovative conclusions after a review of relevant literature and the journal you're submitting to prides itself on publishing traditional scholarship – just the sort of journal, by the way, in which such conclusions might have maximum effect – emphasise in your letter how your research is based upon a careful review of the scholarly tradition. If your paper compares surgical treatments of an ailment with nonsurgical treatments and the journal you think the best fit for it focuses on surgery, highlight the surgical aspect of your work in your covering letter, whether the results you present favour surgical methods or not (for more advice on writing a covering letter to accompany your submission, see Section 6.1 of this *Guide*).

You can also increase your chances of publishing success by using specialised terminology with precision and extreme care. Only use such specialised terminology if it is entirely appropriate to your topic and do not overuse it. If the specialised terms you use are associated with the journal's area of specialisation, you can use them fairly freely with the assumption that your readers will understand them (which doesn't mean, by the way, that you can avoid using terminology precisely or defining abbreviations: see especially

Sections 4.2 & 4.4.1), but any terminology you use whether in the paper or any accompanying documents that may not be familiar to those readers or to the editor or reviewers of the journal should be carefully explained.

Your title is essential as well, and should ideally be worded to prioritise the journal's primary concerns as well as your own, and your abstract can similarly highlight the journal's focuses while clearly outlining the nature of your work and its importance. Writing such effective titles and abstracts is no easy task, of course, but many an editor never makes it past the abstract of papers that are quickly rejected, and it's essential to provide an abstract for your paper that makes a journal editor (as well as its reviewers and readers) respect your scholarship, understand its importance and see it as entirely appropriate for that publication (for advice on writing academic and scientific titles and abstracts, see Section 6.2). It goes without saying that title, abstract, and all other aspects of the paper should conform in every way possible to the author guidelines provided by the journal, though to be honest it seems this can never be said enough (and much of Chapter 3 of this *Guide* is dedicated to the topic). Submission procedures should also be noted and followed precisely (see Section 6.3 below), and the language in which you write your paper should be clear, correct, professional and, if possible, eloquent (see especially Chapter 4). Finally, your paper itself and all additional files you submit along with it should be carefully proofread and polished to the highest textual shine you can manage.

As you prepare your paper, consider the editor's perspective – as much as you can anticipate it. This will help you earn positive attention from a respected and influential journal, and it's well worth working to meet the requirements of such a journal because one truly valuable scholarly article published in a highly rated academic or scientific journal is worth far more (and looks far better on your CV) than two or three adequate papers published in second- or third-rate journals.

18

PRS Tip:
Some journals will dedicate a particular issue or volume to a specific theme, and solicit articles that fit under the rubric of that theme. In such situations, you should only submit your paper for consideration in that issue or volume if your paper clearly deals with the theme specified, and you should also explain in your covering letter why and how your paper addresses that theme. Although it is generally a waste of time to submit an article that is off topic in such cases, submissions that share a topic or approach can result in a thematic trend in any given issue or volume of a journal, and many journals will welcome cohesive content of this sort. So if you have colleagues or (fellow) students involved in research similar to your own who are also preparing papers for publication, it can be a good strategy to submit your papers to the same journal around the same time. It won't guarantee acceptance, of course, but if a journal receives more than one paper on the same or a similar topic, the connections may inspire a theme-oriented issue in which papers on that theme will stand a somewhat better chance of achieving publication. It's another way to stack the deck in your favour as you submit your paper.

Part II:
Preparing, Presenting and Polishing Your Work

CHAPTER 3
Deciphering Journal Guidelines and Designing an Effective Presentation

Paradoxically, successfully following the author guidelines or instructions provided by academic and scientific journals (usually on their web sites) can be both the simplest and most complicated aspect of preparing a scholarly paper for publication. If your first language is not English and you're dealing with author instructions written in English, following the guidelines becomes even more complicated because exactly what is meant can sometimes be tricky to decipher even for native English speakers. The requirements differ from journal to journal, sometimes slightly and at others enormously, and some journals provide extremely detailed instructions about almost every part or feature of a paper, while others are far more general and leave much about presentation up to the author. No matter how small or insignificant a detail requested by a journal may seem, however, it should be treated with great importance. If, for instance, a journal's guidelines call for a 10-point Times New Roman font with 1.3 line spacing but 1.8 before headings, which should be in a 12-point font, don't question it – simply adjust the format of your paper to conform to the requirements. The journal would not have given such detailed instructions if this format weren't important, and it's much easier to comply than to have your paper rejected simply because you think such details unimportant or even because you have a better reason, such as considering a 10-point font too small for readers or preferring double spacing for clarity.

PART II: PREPARING, PRESENTING AND POLISHING YOUR WORK

Journal guidelines can also be helpful in ways not necessarily intended by the journal. For example, if the guidelines use 'e-mail' (with a hyphen rather than without one), the hyphenated form is almost certainly the best one to use in your paper. Do be careful, however, because journal guidelines can be as inconsistent as other texts online ('e-mail' may be used in one paragraph and 'email' in the next), so keep your eyes open to such inconsistencies, which can also crop up in the specific instructions offered to authors. You might have just determined, for instance, from the description of referencing formats provided in a set of guidelines that you definitely need a full stop after each date in a reference list, only to discover that the very next example provided by the journal does not use one. In such cases, you can always consult articles already published by the journal to see how their authors dealt successfully with such confusing instructions, but in the end a decision about which format will be best in your own paper will need to be made, and whether you choose to use that full stop or not, it's essential to be consistent and use the same format throughout your paper.

Indeed, as with so many other aspects of preparing academic or scientific writing for publication, a combination of accuracy and consistency is the name of the game when following journal guidelines. Many scholars consider matters of presentation and formatting secondary to the research, results and argument of a paper, and in literal terms, this is true: without the content of a paper, there is nothing to format or present. Whether the format of an article is considered a priority by academics and scientists or not, however, effective formatting can greatly increase the clarity of a paper and it is most certainly a priority for the editors of journals: were it not, there would be no point in providing instructions for authors. Formatting is the most visible aspect of a paper and can be checked at a glance, which means that it is often used by editors as a measure of many other elements of a paper that take much more time to identify and judge. By ignoring author guidelines and presenting your work in an inappropriate, incorrect or inconsistent format, you provide an overworked editor inundated with stacks of submissions the opportunity to clear one more piece of work off his or her desk, often without even reading your abstract.

The assumption that there is a correlation between the quality of scholarship in a paper and the quality of its presentation is not always correct – good scholarship can be hidden in poorly prepared papers, after all, and beautifully presented work can contain poor scholarship – but there is nonetheless truth in the idea that an author who can accurately and consistently follow instructions and format his or her paper just as the journal would have it is also an academic or scientist who reads and refers to sources and reports methods and results in accurate and meaningful ways. Exactitude and precision are, after all, not just required by journals, but also elements of quality scholarship, and there is no doubt that many editors think about guidelines and scholarship in precisely these ways: a well-organised paper heralds a well-organised mind. Such compliance on the part of authors also indicates to an editor their willingness to be accommodating and work effectively with the journal to achieve successful publication. So the primary message here is to make your paper look as good to the journal you've chosen for submission as you believe the work that went into the paper is – you've put lot of time and effort into writing your article, so it certainly deserves the chance to shine.

3.1 Titles, Headings and Subheadings: Not Just Fancy Words

Although journals differ in the amount of detail they provide about the kind of titles, headings and subheadings they want authors to use, most journals offer some instructions on how to format these elements, and since headings in general are probably the single most immediately visible aspect of your paper, following those instructions to the letter is vital. If a journal's guidelines ask that the title contain no more than 80 characters, use capitals for the first letter of both the title and the subtitle and include no abbreviations, then your title should observe all of these requirements. If the guidelines indicate that the abstract should be divided into sections using particular headings in italic font with each followed by a colon also in italic font, then you should format your abstract in precisely this way. If the guidelines insist that all first-level headings should appear in 14-point bold font and sport capitals on every main word, all second-level headings should appear in 12-point italics with only the first letter uppercase, and all third-level headings should be in bold font and tucked into the beginning of paragraphs as a short sentence and followed by a full stop (also in bold), then your headings should use these formats consistently and accurately.

In many cases, the headings themselves, especially for the first level, will be specified in the journal guidelines as well: Background, Methodology, Results, Discussion and Conclusions, for instance. If this is the case with the journal to which you're submitting your paper, you should do your very best to use these headings. If absolutely necessary, you can add a colon and brief subtitle to designated headings – Background: Previous Trials and Literature, for example, or Methodology: Participants and Questionnaires – but these extra words can instead become subheadings or second-level headings, with *Participants* and *Questionnaires*, for instance, as subsections within the main **Methodology** section of your paper. The latter would be the safer route in most cases, and since very few journals require particular wording for headings beneath first-level headings, there will generally be more flexibility in choosing your second-level and subsequent headings.

It will come as a great relief to some authors that many journals do not give such detailed instructions about the format or wording of headings – many, for example, will simply limit authors to using three levels of heading beyond the title. This means that you have the opportunity to devise a creative heading for each section that accurately reflects the content of the section it introduces, and to format the three levels of headings as you wish, but it doesn't mean that the headings can be laid out or formatted in a careless or inconsistent manner. If, for instance, you simply type all your headings in using the exact same font and format, then your reader (including that all-important editor at the journal) will not be able to distinguish a second-level heading from a first-level or third-level one. So the freedom to format your headings as you like is an opportunity to flaunt your creative formatting skills: use bold font for the first level, italics for the second and regular font for the third, or perhaps larger bold font for the first level, a smaller font in bold for the second and the smaller font in italics for the third. The possibilities are virtually endless, but be sure that the system you design works effectively to distinguish all the sections of your paper, and once you've decided on the format and levels you'll be using, be consistent and stick to your system.

Authors are generally so steeped in their own work that it's difficult to be fully aware of the confusion that can result when headings are used in inconsistent ways. Certainly headings are fancy words and make your paper more visually attractive, but they are also essential to the clarity of your argument and all the information contained within it. If, for instance, in the second of the examples I've provided in the preceding paragraph – first level: large bold, second level: small bold and third level: small italics – the reader comes across two headings in a row in small bold font without any text between them, what is he or she to make of the structure of the paper? Are the two headings equivalent and, if so, is there text missing between them? Should the anomaly be read in some other way or has the author simply neglected to format these headings appropriately? A different kind of confusion arises if the reader comes across a heading in large italics or regular font, neither of which fit into the system the author has established with the first few headings. Is a fourth level of heading intended or is the format simply an error for one of the three levels already used? Such inconsistencies not only introduce glaring errors of the kind that editors are seeking, they force the reader to conjecture about the structure of the paper and can also be misleading and even promote misinterpretation of the work you're submitting.

So be creative with your headings while you're following journal guidelines, work to lay your paper out in an attractive way that clarifies the progress or stages of your argument, and don't be afraid to use space as well as different fonts to distinguish heading levels. A large heading in bold font seems to demand a somewhat larger space above it than does a small heading in italics, and such effective spacing can render the structure of your paper even more successful for your readers. As an art historian friend of mine once said when looking over my CV for me, "try to leave a little more space on the page." She saw that space as a vital component of the document – one that rendered it more attractive and user friendly – and if a journal's guidelines indicate any spacing requirements, they are equally vital. When a journal asks you to use double line spacing, for instance, which tends to be the most common spacing requested, it's because those who will be working with your text find this format the most efficient, so there's no reason not to comply, and spacing above and below headings can be adjusted for an effective layout no matter what basic line spacing you're using.

Some journals will ask you to number your sections and subsections, while others will very specifically ask you not to do so. If the guidelines you're working with do call for numbered sections, they will almost certainly require the numbering of subsections as well, with the most standard format as follows: **1. Methodology** (first level), *1.1 Participants* and *1.2 Questionnaires* (second level), and 1.2.1 The First Questionnaire and 1.2.2 The Second Questionnaire (third level). Be sure to use after the numbers the punctuation required by the journal – occasionally, for instance, a colon instead of a full stop will be wanted – and beware of automatically numbering your sections in a program such as Microsoft Word (for more on automatic formatting, see Section 5.3). This function can produce a tidy layout, of course, but it can also introduce errors based on the way in which you type material into your document by deciding that one of your numbered headings should not be included in what it sees as a numbered list. This will result in misnumbering, and the problem can be magnified if you have several levels of subheadings, bringing disorder to your efforts to achieve careful organisation. So it's always best to number your sections manually and maintain control over your paper's structure. It's also best to use the numbers of sections where referring to them within your paper, and if your sections aren't numbered, to make any cross references as specific as possible, using the exact wording of headings whenever you can.

Finally, a few journals will even set specific word limits for each section of a paper, or suggest that each section should be a single paragraph. This requirement is more difficult to comply with, but it, too, must be taken seriously, so if you find that you simply have too much information to fit into the word limits for a single section, you may need to engage in a little creative division and devise additional headings to find a compromise between the journal guidelines and the nature of your research and paper.

PRS Tip:
One of the best ways to improve your use headings of all kinds in the scholarly papers you write is to pay careful attention to how headings are used in the many books and papers you read. This will be especially helpful in the case of papers published by the journal to which you're hoping to submit your own paper, of course, but it's also good to be aware of how headings are laid out to deal with the challenges presented by the contents of any text. To enable topics to be located in this Guide, for instance, there are four levels of heading under the title, with each level numbered differently for precise cross-referencing: part headings appear in a large blue font with Roman numerals (Part I, Part II, etc.), chapter titles in a bold font with Arabic numerals (Chapter 1, Chapter 2, etc.), chapter sections in a bold font with both chapter and section numbers (1.1, 1.2, etc.) and chapter subsections in a regular font with chapter, section and subsection numbers (4.4.1, 4.4.2, etc.).

3.2 Paragraphs and Lists: Effective Presentation and Transition

3.2.1 Structured and Fully Developed Paragraphs

As mentioned at the end of Section 3.1, a few journals will recommend how long paragraphs on particular subjects or in particular sections should be, but as a general rule journal guidelines rarely offer any advice about how to write well-structured and fully developed paragraphs. They don't neglect this aspect of writing because they don't expect it, however; it is more likely that there is an unspoken assumption that any author submitting his or her writing to a respected academic or scientific journal will already know how write perfect paragraphs. This isn't always the case, however, and particularly for those working in a language not their own or those new to the publishing game, writing effective paragraphs can be something of a challenge, so a bit of practical advice seems in order here. One important fact to remember is that a single sentence does not make a paragraph. This doesn't mean that a single sentence cannot stand alone, but that it should only do so if the context and information justify such special treatment.

Let's say, for instance, that you have a number of sentences with each of them outlining the results of a particular test or method of analysis. In such cases, authors often format each sentence as a separate paragraph, most likely because such a structure separates and therefore clarifies the information. This isn't incorrect and the odd journal will even ask for such data to be separated in this way. In addition, short paragraphs (like short sentences) can be a great deal more effective than overly long ones, but strictly speaking, a paragraph focuses on developing a single idea, so that string of single-sentence paragraphs reporting results can, in many cases, be gathered into a single paragraph that discusses the results of the analytical tests conducted in a study. If you find that you only have a sentence worth of information to report regarding each test, it's a good idea to cluster the data together in this way, and if the information proves too much for a single paragraph, it can be divided into two or more paragraphs with each one focussing on tests of a similar nature or tests that rendered similar results. Paragraph writing is far from an exact science, of course, but strictly speaking the first sentence should introduce the idea, the following sentences should develop it in any number of ways and the last sentence should bring the paragraph to an effective close, ideally in a way that guides your reader on to the next paragraph.

Paragraphs that are too long can be problematic as well, particularly because they tend to merge and develop a number of ideas instead of separating them for clarity and therefore can lack logical interconnection or coherence. Long paragraphs are often associated with complex thought and interrelated ideas, which is exactly what one wants to see in an academic or scientific article, but paragraphs that run on too long and become jumbled can obscure the ideas presented and lose the attention of readers, who do not know your material as well as you do. By breaking long paragraphs into shorter paragraphs, you provide your readers with visual and intellectual breaks that offer them the chance to assimilate the idea(s) you've just discussed before moving on the next, and you also make it easier for them to find material again when needed. Finally, you create a more effective structure for the complex ideas you're discussing, which can improve and clarify the information you're sharing and thus the progression of your overall argument.

Organising your paper into effective paragraphs will only be successful, however, if the transitions between your paragraphs are smooth and clear. If you are shifting to a different topic or focussing on a different study as you begin a new paragraph, you need to make that absolutely clear by explaining the transition. Use specific discourse markers indicating a change of topic, a comparison or contrast, or a focus on a different study or text or experiment, and repeat whatever words are necessary at the beginning of a new paragraph to connect it logically to the paragraph before it. Pronouns such as 'it,' 'this' and 'they' should be avoided at the beginning of a new paragraph: even if the antecedent is obvious, starting a paragraph with a pronoun is simply poor style in English, and when the antecedent is not obvious, it's extremely difficult for your reader to determine exactly what you're talking about. Use a noun or noun phrase instead to identify your subject at the beginning of a new paragraph and you'll find that not only your paragraphs, but the logical movement of your paper as a whole will benefit (on the use of pronouns, see also Section 4.4.3).

3.2.2   Using Lists Effectively

Some journals provide advice on formatting lists, but it's rare. Those that do tend to offer very specific guidelines, asking authors to use bulleted lists or not, to use numbers or letters instead of bullets depending on the placement of a list (within the body of a paragraph or separate), or to use a full stop or a semi-colon after each item depending on the length and grammatical nature of the items. If instructions of this kind are provided, read them carefully and follow them precisely – the journal editors wouldn't have bothered to provide all those details if they didn't want lists formatted exactly as they describe.

In most cases, however, such instructions won't be provided and you will need to figure out for yourself how best to present information in lists, and whatever methods you choose as most effective for the information you need to present, balance and parallelism will be essential. This is to say that each item in the list should be worded and structured as similarly to other items in the list as possible. If the first item begins with a noun followed by a verb (e.g., 'satisfaction is guaranteed'), then it's best not to word the second item with a participle followed by a noun (e.g., 'guaranteeing satisfaction'). Instead, adjust the wording so that every item in your list uses a similar structure, especially if the list as a whole forms a sentence, in which case the sentence must be complete and grammatically correct. Always be sure to observe correct grammar as much as possible, and if the items in your list are long, it's best to use a full sentence (or more than one) for each item. In this way, your lists will function effectively whether they're incorporated into a sentence in your text or separated in a bulleted list with several sentences in each item.

In all cases, you should take special care to introduce any lists you use by explaining exactly what is laid out in each list and making the transition between your prose and your list smooth and effective. For example, if you're about to list categories of personality traits considered in the participants in your study, make the function of the list explicit by introducing it with something like 'The following personality categories were considered in this study,' using a colon after it and presenting the list immediately. Lists can be extremely effective ways of presenting or reporting complex information in clear and accessible ways, but only if they are formatted and introduced in a manner that makes their function and content absolutely clear to your readers, and if their grammar and syntax are correct and effective in relation to both content and good English (see also Section 4.4.1, and, for automatic formatting in lists, Section 5.3).

PRS Tip:
The proofreaders at PRS read a lot of academic and scientific writing in a wide variety of disciplines and specialisations, so we've kind of seen it all when it comes to the presentation and layout of scholarly articles – the good, the bad and the ugly. As readers who need to understand the texts before us both quickly and thoroughly, we can attest to just how vital the use of informative, distinctive and consistent headings, the logical development of thoughtful paragraphs, the clear explanation of transitions and the effective construction of lists are to your readers' understanding of your research and argument. Noticing when aspects of your writing aren't working to improve communication or are in fact hindering it is precisely what we do, so we can offer suggestions and corrections to help you produce a carefully organised and beautifully presented article that looks as good as it reads.

PART II: PREPARING, PRESENTING AND POLISHING YOUR WORK

CHAPTER 4
Journal Guidelines and Formal Scholarly English

Although many aspects of an academic or scientific article can contribute to readers' misunderstanding or misinterpreting your work, your writing style and the accuracy of the language you use are of paramount importance to successful communication. All scholarly journals publishing articles in the English language will want (and the guidelines provided by most of them will specify the need for) articles written in English that is both clear and correct. Many will recommend using a professional proofreader who is proficient in the English language, especially if you are not a native English speaker. Before sending your work to a proofreader, however, you will need to do everything you possibly can to make your language and style as clear, correct, precise and consistent as possible because even a talented and experienced proofreader will only be able to help you communicate effectively if you do so well enough that he or she can get a good idea of what you're trying to say. The use of excellent English will in any case benefit both you and your article as you work through all the stages of publication, from emailing editors to proofreading the final copyedited version of your paper.

4.1   British versus American English

The guidelines of some journals will indicate specific requirements regarding language and it's essential that your writing style follows these instructions carefully. The most common specification among many English journals is the use of either British or American English, and even those journals that allow both kinds will not want to see a mixture of British and American spellings in the same paper. Differences between the two forms of English include 'ou' in British versus 'o' in American (British: 'colour' and 'behaviour'; American: 'color' and 'behavior'), 're' in British versus 'er' in American (British: 'theatre'; American: 'theater'), doubling of consonants in British versus single consonants in American (British: 'modelling' and 'focussed'; American: 'modeling' and 'focused') and '-ise' endings in

British versus '-ize' endings in American (British: 'analyse' and 'recognising'; American: 'analyze' and 'recognizing'). The last of these differences is no longer observed as strictly as it once was, and '-ize' endings are now acceptable in British English as well, at least as far as some journals and publishers are concerned. There are other differences as well (e.g., 'oe' in British vs. 'e' in American: 'manoeuvre' vs. 'maneuver') and certain inconsistencies that can be unpredictable ('parameter' and 'compromise,' for example, are the same in both British and American), but the spell check function of Word can help if you set the language as UK or US English. The program won't do it all for you, however, and do be aware that it's not always reliable, but many dictionaries will provide alternate spellings, so if you're unsure about a word, take the time to look it up.

4.2   Understanding Abbreviations

The guidelines provided by most journals will have something to say about the use of abbreviations. Some frown upon them and ask authors to keep their use to a bare minimum or to use only standard abbreviations for measures. Others will expect you to use abbreviations, but give very specific instructions about how they should be introduced, defined, used with consistency and provided in an alphabetical list as well as in the text. If the journal to which you're submitting your paper offers such specific instructions, follow them carefully, but even if the guidelines say virtually nothing about using abbreviations, there are useful and effective ways of using abbreviations that should be observed in all cases for two important reasons: to maintain conventional professional standards and to ensure that your readers will understand your abbreviations and thus what you are saying about the terms and concepts you abbreviate.

Standard abbreviations of measures can be found in a number of places, such as the American Psychological Association (APA) and other style manuals and many dictionaries, and generally do not need to be defined in your paper. So the important point with such abbreviations is to use the appropriate format for each and use it in the exact same format each and every time the abbreviation is used: 'ms' for millisecond, for example, not 'ms' in one instance and 'msec' in the next; 'kph' and 'mph,' not 'km/hr' and 'mph.' The same is the case with common Latin abbreviations such as 'etc.,' 'e.g.,' 'i.e.,' 'cf.,' 'vs.' and 'viz.' If you're going to use them, do so with complete consistency. Technically speaking, none of these Latin abbreviations needs to be in italics and the full stops should appear where I've placed them here, but some guidelines will vary this slightly by using italics or eliminating the full stops, so it's always worth checking. As a general rule of good style, these Latin abbreviations should be used only in parenthetical material (i.e., inside parentheses): main sentences that use 'e.g.,' 'i.e.' and 'cf.' often become incomprehensible, especially if the writer isn't entirely sure exactly what the abbreviations mean ('cf.,' for instance, which is misused more often than not, means 'compare,' not 'see'). So write out exactly what you mean in your main sentences, and when you do use these Latin abbreviations parenthetically, be sure you know what they mean and use them correctly.

The Latin abbreviations 'et al.,' 'ibid.,' 'loc. cit.' and 'op. cit.' are generally used in the context of reference lists, footnotes, endnotes and citations. The last two – 'loc. cit.' and 'op. cit.' – tended to be confusing even when they were widely used, and thankfully have been virtually abandoned in modern scholarship, so you're most likely to find guidelines warning against their use than instructing authors on how to use them: certainly, they're best avoided. 'Ibid.,' on the other hand, is still used in footnote and endnote references in the humanities. It abbreviates 'ibidem,' which means 'in the same place' or 'in that very place,' so is used instead of repeating bibliographical information when a source is cited immediately after it has been cited in the preceding note (or sentence within a note). Because it means 'in that very place,' it must be used with great care: only if everything about the second citation is exactly the same as the first can it be used alone. For example, if the reference in footnote 1 is 'Smith, *Amadeus*, p. 4' and you need to cite the same author, book and page number in footnote 2, then 'ibid.' can be used alone, but if you're citing the same author and book in footnote 2 with a different page number, then the page number should be added: 'ibid., p. 7.' Never use 'ibid.' if its meaning is potentially unclear:

if, for instance, you've cited two sources in footnote 1 and you use 'ibid.' in footnote 2, your readers will not be able to tell which source you mean by 'ibid.' In such cases more detail must be provided – 'Smith, ibid.,' for example – or the use of 'ibid.' should be avoided altogether.

The meaning of 'idem' and 'eadem' is similar, so although they're not abbreviations, they should be considered along with these referencing abbreviations. They both mean 'the same,' with 'idem' being the masculine form and 'eadem' the feminine, and although they tend to appear in English dictionaries (especially 'idem') so don't need to be in italic font, they are often italicised. They are used predominantly in footnotes and endnotes when an author who has just been cited is immediately cited a second time. For example, if you've just cited 'Smith, *Amadeus*, p. 4' and you're now citing 'Smith, *Beethoven*, p. 8,' you can use 'idem, *Beethoven*, p. 8' if Smith is a man or 'eadem, *Beethoven*, p. 8' if Smith is a woman. As with 'ibid.,' however, these Latin terms need to be used only when it's absolutely clear which author is being cited, and if there is any potential for confusion, don't use them. Since many journals don't encourage the use of such Latin shortcuts, it's also a good idea to check the journal guidelines and only use them if their use is specified as acceptable.

The Latin abbreviation 'et al.' is used in virtually all academic and scientific journals when referring to authors of a multi-author work. It abbreviates 'et alii' (masculine), 'et aliae' (feminine) or 'et alia' (neuter, although this meaning isn't really relevant for authors, who are necessarily men or women rather than objects without gender). All of these Latin terms mean 'and the others' and because 'et' is the complete Latin word for 'and,' a full stop should never follow the 'et' part. A full stop should follow 'al.,' however, but do check the journal guidelines or style manual you're following because some will call for 'et al' without the final full stop and some will require the use of italics on the abbreviation. Generally speaking, 'et al.' is the only one of these Latin abbreviations that can be used in the main text of formal academic or scientific prose as well as in parenthetical material: 'Jackson et al. (2013) argued that...' or 'In this study (Jackson et al., 2013) it is argued that....' (on the use of 'et al.,' see also Section 5.2.1).

The most notorious of abbreviations is the acronym, an abbreviation made up of the first letters of all the words or only the main words in a name or term: WHO for the World Health Organization is a well-known example. With the exception of a few acronyms that are better known than the terms they abbreviate – IQ and AIDS, for instance – each acronym you use in your paper should be formally introduced by presenting the full version of the term or name along with the abbreviated version (in parentheses) before the acronym is ever used on its own: 'the World Health Organization (WHO) reported….' Make sure that you position the abbreviated form to represent accurately exactly what the acronym abbreviates – 'the critical time gap (CTG) test revealed…,' not 'the critical time gap test (CTG) revealed…' – and that your subsequent use of the acronym reflects that placement (CTG meaning 'critical time gap' but not 'test' as well). If you use an acronym for a corporate author in an in-text citation (WHO, 2012), you can simply introduce the full term and acronym in reverse order in the reference list: WHO (World Health Organization) instead of World Health Organization (WHO). This ensures that your reader will be able to find the reference easily in your list, but also provides complete bibliographical information. If you do not follow these simple procedures when using acronyms, your reader may not know what you're talking about – a frustrating experience for both author and reader. Once an acronym has been introduced in this manner, however, you can use it with confidence knowing that you'll be understood, so long as you use it accurately and consistently. Many journals will ask that an acronym be used in all cases instead of the full term once it's been introduced, and that acronyms not be introduced and used at all unless they're used with considerable frequency.

There are a number of other concerns that you should also consider when using acronyms and other abbreviations. For instance, sometimes a plural term such as United Nations is abbreviated with an acronym that doesn't show the plural nature of the full version (UN), but if you're going to use an abbreviation for both singular and plural forms of a term, add an 's' when you intend the plural of the original – KI for 'key informant' but KIs for 'key informants.' In such cases, make sure that you use the appropriate form (singular or plural) when you introduce and define the abbreviation – 'My key informants (KIs) were...,' not 'My key informants (KI) were...' – and that the language you use around the acronym when it's used alone reflects the difference: 'My KIs were...,' not 'My KIs was...' (the use of that 's' will help with this). Generally speaking, abbreviations of all kinds should be avoided in the headings and subheadings of your paper, even if they've already been introduced and defined, and some journals will ask that they be avoided in the abstract of a paper as well. If you do have to use abbreviations in your abstract, defining them there does not mean you can avoid doing so in the main paper – they will need to be introduced and defined in both places (on the use of abbreviations and acronyms in the tables, figures, title, abstract and keywords of an academic or scientific paper, see Sections 5.1 & 6.2 below).

4.3   Punctuating Appropriately

Pause and Effect, the title of an acclaimed book on the punctuation of late-medieval manuscripts,[1] neatly summarises a primary function of punctuation: punctuation tells your reader when to 'pause' and can have an enormous 'effect' on the ability of your prose to communicate your thoughts clearly. Punctuation has a number of other functions as well, and can mean the difference between your carefully crafted sentences functioning successfully or failing. Sentences that lack necessary punctuation or use punctuation incorrectly can end up saying something very different from what you intended. There is no one set of universal rules to follow when punctuating English prose, however, and each sentence, whether long or short, laden with parenthetical clauses or straight to the point, is a unique construct that must be punctuated individually and with care. As with so many other aspects of an academic or scientific paper, effective punctuation requires precision and consistency, and there are some basic principles and patterns that should be observed.

First, take care to read whatever the journal's guidelines may say about punctuation. It's rare to find much if any advice on punctuation

---

[1] Malcolm Parkes, *Pause and Effect: Punctuation in the West* (Berkeley, CA: University of California Press, 1993).

in author instructions, but there are instances of very specific requirements. The use of a comma before 'and' in lists of three or more items is an example: some journals will want the comma ('birds, butterflies, and bees') and some will not ('birds, butterflies and bees'); if a journal's guidelines bother to advise authors either way, take that advice to heart and apply it consistently. The use of a comma in conjunction with an 'and' that opens an additional independent clause in a sentence comes to mind as another punctuation issue I've seen addressed in journal guidelines. Further advice on this and other punctuation usage patterns is sometimes provided in academic and scientific style manuals as well (APA, Chicago, etc.), so if the journal you're submitting your paper to recommends using a particular style, familiarise yourself with the punctuation rules laid out in the corresponding manual.

When it comes down to the nitty-gritty of punctuating your paper, however, you'll need to decide which patterns will work best to communicate your research and argument. Once you've chosen the patterns you'll use – a comma or not before that 'and' in lists, for instance – be consistent in all similar constructions. Only if you need to change your usual practice to increase the clarity of a sentence (or decrease the risk of misinterpretation) should you vary the pattern (by using a comma before that 'and' in lists when absolutely necessary, for instance, even though as a general rule you do not). While you're refining your punctuation practices, it might be helpful to keep a few basics in mind:

- Remember that a dependent clause opening a sentence (and in other positions as well) should usually be followed by a comma (e.g., 'According to Smith, these results...'), although shorter clauses can function well without one (e.g., 'In 2003 the numbers increased...').
- Full stops are always used at the end of a sentence, and they should be placed inside (to the left of) footnotes, outside (to the right of) parenthetical citations, and either inside or outside Vancouver-style numerical references, depending on journal guidelines.

- The function of a colon (:) is entirely different from that of a semi-colon (;) and the two are frequently confused: a colon heralds an example or several examples (often in the form of a list or quotation) or an explanation of what has just been stated (just as the colon in this sentence does); a semi-colon, on the other hand, is (as it is in this sentence) rather like a large comma, separating independent sections of a long and complex sentence (or sometimes the items of a list that forms a long sentence) in places where a comma simply won't sufficiently clarify the sentence structure and meaning.
- Hyphenation can be incredibly tricky because dictionaries, style manuals and sometimes journal guidelines can all indicate different patterns and rules – 'intersubjectivity' or 'inter-subjectivity,' 'nonsignificant' or 'non-significant,' 'reintroduce' or 're-introduce' and so on. If the journal you're submitting to does not provide specific instructions or a specific style (such as Chicago) to follow, the best policy is to adopt a system and stick to it, remembering that certain compounds should always be hyphenated: when two vowels would end up back to back without the hyphen (re-establish), when confusion could result were the term closed ('re-create,' which has a different meaning than 'recreate'), when the second element bears a capital (non-English) or is a numeral (pre-1990s), and when a compound adjective appears before a noun (a 'well-known theory' but a 'theory that is well known').
- Finally, although indicated by tiny apostrophes that can get lost at times, possessives should always be accurately punctuated with the general rule being that the apostrophe appears before the 's' in the singular form (student's) and after it in the plural (students'), though there are, as always in English, exceptions: 'men's,' for example, which does not use an 's' for the plural form, so the 's' is there solely to indicate the possessive and the apostrophe appears before it. Try not to overuse possessives: particularly in their plural form, they can become awkward in English, so it's often best to write out a phrase using 'of' instead of stacking possessives: 'the participants' fathers' occupations,' for instance, is clearer and more elegant as 'the occupations of the participants' fathers.'

On the use of quotation marks, see Section 5.2.1 below.

PRS Tip:
It's amazing how details can be right before the eyes and still slip past unnoticed, but such is the case with incorrect punctuation, familiar abbreviations and spelling variations. Sometimes this is because the detail is small and unobtrusive: a full stop is tiny, after all, and a semi-colon looks much like a colon when there's no time to do more than glance at it. At other times it's due to not knowing – everyone has to look up the differences between American and British English at times. At still other times such negligence is paradoxically caused by knowing the material too well: I've seen more than one paper in which an author works to define every acronym that's used once or twice (and even some that aren't used again at all), only to neglect providing a definition for an abbreviation that's unusual, used 50 or 100 times in the paper and absolutely central to the data and argument. A classic case of being so immersed in one's own work that it becomes difficult to see what the audience might need, this forces a guessing game on readers (except those lucky enough to know the meaning already) and leads to frustration and potential misunderstanding. Fortunately, the PRS proofreading team has many eyes well trained in the detection of such problems, and the time to attend to them thoroughly and with precision.

4.4   Finding Your Scholarly Voice

Although any author should work to establish a voice of authority when writing, this is nowhere more important than in academic and scientific prose: as a scholarly writer, you need to assume a professional stance and sound in every way like you know exactly what you're talking about. In order to do this, it's essential that you do know what you're talking about, of course, but it's entirely possible to know your subject intimately and work very hard to express the most profound of thoughts about it only to fail because certain aspects of the language and phrasing you use come across to your readers as awkward, imprecise or unprofessional. Attending to all the issues raised above – accurate and effective punctuation, appropriate use of abbreviations, consistent adherence to British or American spelling, complete sentences organised into well-developed paragraphs, a well-planned paper using sound sources and methods to construct a meaningful argument, and so on – contributes to a written voice that speaks with professional authority, but there are a number of other matters, some of them seemingly small details, that often prove problematic and can literally make or break a paper by either engaging and convincing or losing and annoying readers.

4.4.1   Vocabulary: Formality, Precision and Variety

A scholarly written voice is necessarily a formal written voice – not quite as formal as it once was, of course, but the principle remains. This means that everything about the language you use in a paper you're preparing for publication in an academic or scientific journal should be absolutely correct, precise and professional in grammatical, syntactic and orthographic terms. Although once as basic as methods and results, formality has become especially challenging in a climate of digital social networking that encourages the use of informal (and often incorrect) language and tends to suggest particularly to younger scholars that such informalities are equally acceptable beyond the realm of tweeting and text messaging. They are not and should be strictly avoided in formal academic or scientific prose, including CVs, proposals and job applications, as well as research papers, theses and scholarly books. The rewards of polishing your writing skills are significant, and there's always the possibility of discovering that carefully crafted formal prose is a rather effective means of expressing complex ideas.

One of the easiest and most obvious ways in which to increase the formality as well as the precision of your writing is to choose your vocabulary with special care. This can mean using the exact same word repeatedly or varying your vocabulary, with each of these appropriate in different situations and for different reasons. Adding variety to your vocabulary is essential to producing an eloquent writing style that will hold the interest of readers, and many words in a sentence can easily be changed to create variety without altering meaning. Avoid, for instance, starting every sentence with 'however,' 'therefore,' 'thus,' 'moreover' or 'furthermore' – use these but mix them up in your prose. Use 'particularly' in some instances and 'especially' in others; use 'as well as' instead of 'and' at times, and 'yet' or 'however' instead of 'but.' When reporting results of trials and tests, vary 'showed' with 'revealed' or 'suggested' or 'indicated,' and when comparing ideas, categories and results, use 'more than' and 'less than' as well as 'compared with' and 'contrasted with.' Be careful, however, when eliminating words to vary your language. For example, in 'pink shirts were given to 12 of the men, but blue to women' the reader easily supplies the verb ('were given') missing from the second half of the sentence and it's also fairly clear that 'blue' stands for 'blue shirts,' but he or she may be wondering 'to what women?' Does the author mean all of the women in the study although only 12 of the men were given shirts? Clearly, more information is needed here, and those of a more traditional persuasion would say that all the missing words should be included when it comes to reporting precise data about methods and results. A more flexible approach is to use enough words (and the right ones) to make your meaning absolutely clear, but you can still vary your language somewhat while doing so: 'but blue ones to the same number of women.'

Be extremely careful when varying (or eliminating) terms that define aspects and elements of your research, methodology and argument or report precise results. In the case of comparison, for instance, be sure to explain with precision the exact details of each side of a comparison or contrast: do not assume that your readers know what you're comparing or contrasting, and do not leave out essential details of the comparison. 'We compared the scores the girls earned in the third trial with the boys' is simply wrong: the scores earned by the girls were no doubt compared with the scores earned by the boys (not the boys themselves), and the boys' scores were probably obtained in a numbered trial as well, so the reader needs more here than the author has provided. Be sure to use the same terms and definitions for the same concepts or categories throughout your paper, especially when those concepts and categories are central to your argument: for example, if you've introduced your study groups as 'surgical group,' 'nonsurgical group' and 'control group,' do not suddenly change that terminology part way through your paper; if your questionnaires are numbered 1, 2 and 3, avoid referring to them without the numbers because this can increase the possibility of unnecessary confusion; and if your study involves participants who are young women and young men, do not call them 'girls' and 'boys' unless they actually are girls and boys (some journals have strict rules about age in relation to these terms, so remember to check the guidelines as well as using common sense with regard to such terms: i.e., people over 20 and usually over 18 are never girls and boys).

All scholars use specialised terminology at times, and certainly such terminology can communicate with a precision that other words simply can't manage. If there's any doubt about your readers' familiarity with the terminology you use in your paper, you will need to take special care to explain it (and the ideas behind it) with precision and as thoroughly as necessary to allow your readers to understand the significance of your methodology and argument. If you're writing for a specialised journal, you can assume an editor (and certainly reviewers) familiar with the terminology associated with the area of specialisation, but you still need to use specialised vocabulary carefully, and never use a smattering of scientific or theoretical terms as a substitute for explaining ideas. The best scholarly writing demonstrates not just a proficiency in using specialised terminology but also a deep understanding of the ideas behind the terminology, and it explains those ideas for its readers while taking them (both ideas and readers) in new directions. Any abbreviations of specialised terminology should be used with the same precision as the original terms, and remember that if you use a list to define terms or outline categories of any kind, your readers will likely return to the list (since lists are particularly easy to locate) in order to review and check the terms you've used if anything does prove confusing, so be especially careful to use those terms and categories in the exact same forms elsewhere in the paper (see also Section 3.2.2 on formatting lists).

Closely related to specialised terminology is the jargon peculiar to a profession or field of study. Such jargon often includes specialised vocabulary, but also tends to use convoluted syntax or awkward word order and can prove to be unintelligible (or very nearly so) to readers. For instance, 'a low young voter turnout election' is simply poor English and not nearly as effective for communicating meaning as 'an election with a low turnout of young voters.' The word 'jargon' is often defined in dictionaries as 'meaningless writing,' 'vague language' or 'gibberish,' none of which the scholarly writer wants in his or her text. Such language is often the result of authors being so immersed in their respective fields of study that they are unaware that they're failing to communicate clearly in plain English, even to many in their own fields, but sometimes I suspect it is used to create an impression of learnedness or mystique. If readers don't understand what they're reading, however, any impression of the author's learning becomes frustrating instead of impressive, and while mystique certainly has its proper place, it is not in a carefully written scholarly article. If you must use jargon, keep it to a minimum and be sure to explain its meaning on first use.

Numbers aren't exactly specialised terminology, but the accurate punctuation (point/full stop, comma or neither) and formatting of numbers (as words or numerals) can be complicated, and all the more so because the rules tend to be very precise yet vary from style to style and journal to journal, so it's essential to consult the guidelines and follow the patterns required in detail. There are, however, a few general rules that reappear frequently across styles and are consistent with the expectations of most academic and scientific journals. They are good, too, to keep in mind if you're not following any particular style or guidelines, but formatting numbers according to your own methods.

- Never start a sentence with a numeral: whatever the number is, it needs to be written out as a word. So it should be 'One participant,' not '1 participant,' and 'Fifty-six men,' not '56 men.' For larger numbers that would be cumbersome to write out (e.g., 14,386), it's best to reword the sentence so it doesn't start with the number.
- Numbers directly associated with measures of any kind should be written as numerals: '4 mm,' '23 cm,' '130 mph,' '8 m' and so on.
- In instances other than the two noted above, numbers 10 and over should be written as numerals ('13 participants,' 'a population of 426 women' and '56 men'), while numbers under 10 should be written as words ('four trials,' 'six students' and 'eight participants').
- Ordinal numbers should follow the same pattern as cardinal numbers: that is, numbers 10 and over should be written as numerals and numbers under 10 should be written as words ('the 56th man in the second trial' and 'the eighth participant in the 77th trial').
- When writing numbers as numerals, be sure to observe English convention – 1,389.09 for 'one thousand, three hundred and eighty-nine point zero nine,' not 1.389,09 – but also check the journal guidelines in case there are any special instructions about using numbers. A few journals will ask for less punctuation, eliminating the comma from the number above (1389.09), for instance.

Finally, formal English prose does not use contractions. Contractions are formed when letters are left out of words and indicated by an apostrophe instead. Examples based on negatives ('not') are especially common – 'don't,' 'doesn't,' 'won't,' 'shouldn't,' 'wouldn't' and 'couldn't' are common examples – and often slip into academic and scientific prose. They won't create confusion, and I use them throughout this *Guide* to produce a casual tone, but 'casual' is not what you want in a formal academic or scientific paper, so contractions should always be avoided. In my experience, scholars don't usually intend to use contractions in their writing, but they are so common and natural in normal speech that they can all too easily creep into writing whenever an author isn't entirely vigilant. So once you have your paper drafted, do a search for apostrophes and expand any contractions that turn up, leaving apostrophes for possessives (or single quotation marks) only.

4.4.2   English Verbs: Tensing Up and Splitting Hairs

If you have at times found yourself cursing the nature of English verbs, you might receive consolation from the fact that you are not alone. Even for native English speakers and writers proficient in the language, English can be a notoriously difficult language to use correctly, more so to use elegantly, and verbs are among the most troublesome aspects of English to negotiate. English verbs are often formed by a combination of separate words ('to understand,' 'will have understood,' 'had understood,' etc.) in a way very different from the conjugation of verbs in other languages. The nuances of the various forms (or tenses) communicate different temporal messages, and the problem is complicated in scholarly prose because referring accurately and effectively to the ideas and results found in sources can be challenging. Tense (present, perfect, pluperfect, etc.) is a key issue, and many a scholarly paragraph reporting information from sources breaks down because the tense of the verbs it uses is inconsistent or does not change according to the nature of the content.

As a general rule, much of what is said in previous scholarship can be referred to in the present tense: for example, 'Jones (1985) argues that...,' 'Parkes (1993) outlines three basic principles' and 'according to Johnson (2010), these results are....' However, if you're comparing or contrasting studies done at different times, you may need to vary the tense you use: 'Jones (1985) argued [perfect] that the problem could not be overcome, but Johnson (2010) sheds [present] new light on the situation.' Often using a compound form with 'has' or 'have' is more effective than a simple past or perfect tense when speaking of scholarly trends or developments: for instance, 'In recent years, many studies have paid far more attention to...' and 'Since the 1990s, there have been several studies that....' However, the studies you're referring to were in fact conducted in the past, so the perfect tense, too, can be correctly used when referring to studies and their authors: for example, 'The study by Jones (1985) explored the migration habits of monarch butterflies' and 'Johnson (2010) investigated the phenomenon by making extensive use of the work of Jones (1985).' As with so much about writing well, there are no hard and fast rules to follow except that it will always help to conceptualise and contextualise clearly in both temporal and intellectual terms the sources and ideas to which you're referring, and adjust your verb forms accordingly.

Among the most troublesome of verb forms in English is the infinitive. In most languages, the infinitive of a verb is a single word: the famous Latin phrase 'veni, vidi, vici' ('I came, I saw, I conquered'), for instance, becomes 'venire, videre, vincere' using the infinitive forms. In English, however, the infinitives of verbs are formed through the addition of 'to' – 'to come, to see, to conquer' – and the two elements of the infinitive ('to' and 'conquer') should no sooner be separated from each other than should the '-ire' or '-ere' ending be separated from the stem of one of the Latin infinitives. There are those, of course, who claim that splitting English infinitives is no longer a concern – even that such fussing over verbs is tantamount to splitting hairs – but I've seen papers returned for revision by the editors of scholarly journals with the specific request to remove or reword all split infinitives, and rightly so. Split infinitives are incorrect grammar and simply not an aspect of formal academic or scientific prose.

However, split infinitives are also all around us daily in our speech and informal written communications, on our radio and television programmes (*Startrek*'s 'to boldly go' is the most famous or infamous, depending on your perspective) and even where we might least expect to find them. Check out, for instance, the descriptive paragraph about *Journal Citation Reports* on the Thomson Reuters web site, which claims that the *Reports* offer 'a systematic, objective means to critically evaluate the world's leading journals' – an unfortunate combination of words that invites the reader 'to evaluate' (the infinitive which is split in this case) with a critical eye the quality of the English used. Infinitives are usually split with an adverb added between the two parts of the verb (as 'boldly' and 'critically' split the infinitives in the examples above), and such split infinitives sometimes sound so natural that they can sneak past the eye of even the most seasoned professional proofreader. At other times the wording of a sentence seems to sound better when the infinitive is split by an adverb: 'boldly to go' and 'to go boldly' simply don't resonate as 'to boldly go' does, probably largely because some of us have heard the last so often that it now seems 'right.' Nonetheless, an adverb should always be removed from amidst an infinitive and either placed elsewhere in the sentence or replaced with alternative wording: for example, 'to evaluate critically' or 'to evaluate with a critical eye.' This will sometimes prove more challenging than it sounds and in certain instances the adverb or adverbial phrase will have to be abandoned altogether to make a sentence work effectively, but as some of the best advice for writers claims, the right verb often doesn't need an adverb to modify it at all, much as the right noun often does not need an adjective.

Another concern when using English verbs arises from the difference between the passive and active voices. In the active voice a subject is clearly stated and the verb is active: 'We investigated the relationship between changing weather patterns and the coverage provided by home insurance policies.' In the passive voice, the object becomes the subject and the verb is passive: 'The relationship between changing weather patterns and the coverage provided by home insurance policies was investigated.' Both are correct English, of course, but because the passive voice does not name the people doing the investigating, it fails to convey with precision who did the research – the authors of the present article as part of the current study, for instance, or a third party (or parties) working at some other time who ought to be cited. Some academic and scientific authors will deliberately use the passive voice in an abstract, perhaps due to a misconception that the passive voice is scholarly, but a scholarly voice is never vague as the passive voice can be, and some journal guidelines will actually ask that the passive voice be avoided, especially in abstracts where precision expressed via as few words as possible is particularly important. So do check the guidelines and when you use the passive voice, do so sparingly and with careful attention to what it actually says and does not say.

4.4.3   Using Pronouns Professionally and Clearly

Pronouns are among the most friendly features of language: they allow the author (or speaker) to say what needs to be said with much greater efficiency and elegance than would be possible were he or she obliged to use the same noun or noun phrase repeatedly even within the same sentence. However, pronouns can also be among the most user-unfriendly features of academic or scientific prose. There are times in creative writing when ambiguity about the meaning of a pronoun is deliberate and effective, but in scholarly writing, the meaning of a pronoun should be obvious and certain (and any rare instances of deliberate ambiguity explained, as I explain the use of 'them' for both ideas and readers in Section 4.4.1 above, or clearly justified by the material). This means that the relationship between a pronoun and its antecedent should be clearly established so that no doubt about the meaning of the pronoun exists. For example, in 'The mother thought the boy was lost. He was actually at a friend's house,' 'He' can only refer to the boy, so there's no risk of confusion. However, in 'The boy lost his old dog Jake. He was actually at a friend's house,' the antecedent of 'He' is not clear. Since the 'boy' is the subject of the first sentence, the reader might expect 'He' to refer to the 'boy,' but it could also refer to the male 'dog Jake,' so confusion is created about what is actually being said, and thus about the implications of the text. Is the dog safe at a friend's house, or did the boy lose the dog at a friend's house and thus in a less familiar and potentially more dangerous landscape? Is there continuing cause for worry or not?

Those examples are extremely simple. When a long and complex sentence reporting and discussing detailed results and conclusions opens with 'It' and contains a couple more instances of that pronoun as well as a 'they' and a 'them,' determining what the author means can become absolutely impossible, especially if that author is also dealing with the challenge of writing in a language not his or her own and perhaps used one 'it' when referring to a plural antecedent and 'they' for a singular one by mistake. In most cases, five pronouns are too many for a sentence in any case, but whether you have many or only one pronoun in a sentence, it is vital that your reader is able to identify the antecedent(s) readily and with certainty. Sometimes the grammar checking function in Word will catch an incorrectly or oddly used pronoun, but much like the spell check function, this is far from reliable. So read your sentences over carefully and whenever you encounter a pronoun, ask yourself if its meaning might possibly be unclear – not to you, but to a reader who can't know what you're saying unless you express your meaning effectively – and if there's any doubt, use a noun or noun phrase instead. Because using pronouns too extensively can tend to distance not only the reader but also the writer from precisely what he or she is saying, analysing your text in this way can actually help you clarify your forms of expression in ways that reach far beyond pronouns, much as writing the meaning of Latin abbreviations out in your text can. Using one thing for another is only a successful policy if both you and your reader know exactly what the replacement represents.

The practice of putting yourself into the shoes of your reader and viewing your own writing from as objective a perspective as you can possibly manage can be surprisingly enlightening and incredibly helpful. If you're able to achieve a little distance from your work, you'll also be able to read it as you might read the scholarly work of colleagues, and while this can assist you with managing far more than pronouns, it will almost always reveal problematic uses of pronouns that contribute to an unprofessional written voice. I am referring specifically here to the use in scholarly prose of the first-person plural pronoun 'we' (and 'us' and 'our' in the other declensions). 'We' can be used with impunity in academic or scientific writing if it refers specifically to the authors, and 'I' is equally acceptable for a single author. In fact, 'I' when used with discretion is often preferable to a third-person circumlocution such as 'the present author' and 'we' more appropriate than, say, 'the present investigators.' The two ('I' and 'we') should not be mixed, however: a paper either has one or more than one author, so it's either 'I' or 'we,' not one in one paragraph and the other in the next. 'We' can also be used successfully (though with care) when referring to researchers or practitioners as a group, such as 'we ethnographers' or 'we as surgeons,' especially when your work relates to methodology and self-awareness.

'We' should not be used in scholarly writing, however, in a general or fictional sense that implicitly includes the readers or even the whole of humanity. Generalising, as any researcher knows, is a dangerous business, and when you include your readers in that 'we,' you also (usually unwittingly) imply that your readers are thinking exactly what you are. Assuming that your readers are thinking as you are can be one of the most certain and instantaneous ways in which to lose your readers' sympathy. 'We can observe that…,' 'We see here…,' 'We now know that…,' 'We human beings do not…' and similar phrases can rapidly become irritating, especially if the author has not provided the results or explanation to shore up the claim. The job of the academic or scientific author is to show, explain, persuade, even defend when necessary with regard to his or her discoveries, but never to assume that the reader is already convinced or to use that assumption as a way in which to develop an argument or as a substitute for scholarly argumentation. 'We observed that…,' 'We saw…,' 'We discovered that…' (with the 'We' applying to the authors in each case) and 'Human participants in this study did not…' all report results, and therefore present evidence and advance an academic or scientific argument. What your readers see or think or discover may or may not do so, and assuming (even unwittingly) that what's going on in your mind is also going on in the minds of your readers often means ignoring the potential for many different responses and interpretations. So while it is good to anticipate the needs of your readers, the best way to meet those needs is to rely on what's going on in your own mind and do your very best to share that clearly and thoughtfully in your writing. So check your use of 'we' carefully as you proofread and revise your paper, and if there's no specific and appropriate antecedent for it, devise a different way to express your thoughts.

'You' should also be avoided in academic and scientific prose. This is rarely a problem for authors as 'we' tends to be, but since I use the second-person voice so frequently in this *Guide* to facilitate concise expression of the advice I'm offering you as an academic or scientific author working toward publication, I thought I best mention it. My practice in this regard is a good example, then, of anticipating the perspective and needs of readers, yet also a classic case of do what I say, but not exactly what I do: in most contexts using 'you' simply establishes too personal a voice for formal academic or scientific writing.

Even the use of 'he,' 'she' and 'they' can be fraught with difficulties, particularly because of the need to avoid gender-specific language. The matter is straightforward when speaking of a male or female subject, but when your language needs to be more general, problems can arise. Some writers would argue that 'they,' 'them' and 'their' are acceptable, non-gender-specific substitutes for the singular forms 'he or she,' 'him or her' and 'his or her.' However, 'they,' 'them' and 'their' are plural, so they are not appropriate or correct with reference to singular nouns, and using them as though they are can quickly become extremely confusing. So when you use something like 'a person,' you need to use a singular pronoun: 'when a person considers the idea, he or she also realises...,' not 'when a person considers the idea, they also realise.' Finally, a human being, person, participant, interviewee, mother, man, teenager or girl is never an 'it,' so do be sure to use 'he,' 'she' or 'they' (or 'him,' 'her' or 'them' in the objective cases and 'his,' 'her' and 'their' in the possessive) when referring to a person. Relative pronouns should be used similarly: 'the man who did that' or 'the participant who scored highest,' not 'the man that did that' or 'the participant that scored highest.'

Such careful usage will not only render your writing clearer and more precise, it will also keep the human element alive in your prose along with scholarly formality. Avoiding the use of a generalising 'we' and a 'you' that's too direct does not mean that you should remove the human element from your prose, and there are a variety of ways to retain this element. Sometimes when reporting complex methods and data while working within tight word limits, an author can let words that assert the presence of human participants in a study fall to the wayside. Most common is the tendency for patients or participants suffering from a particular disease or ailment to be reduced through a kind of shorthand to the disease or ailment. While this sort of language is sometimes necessary to convey results efficiently, it should be avoided as much as possible, and certainly not used when first introducing the participants in your study. Some journals have rather strict guidelines about referring to research participants – some of them even frowning upon the use of 'subjects' instead of 'individuals' or 'people' – so do be sure to check the journal guidelines before making final decisions about such matters.

PRS Tip:
The proofreaders at PRS are well educated in a variety of disciplines and all of us are experts in the English language. We know how a scholarly paper in English should read because we are scholars, and some of us have published our own academic or scientific writing. So there's a great deal we can do to help you make your scholarly voice just what it should be, but it's essential that you do everything you can to ensure that your vocabulary, grammar and syntax are as correct and clear as possible. Remember that if a seasoned professional proofreader familiar with academic and scientific prose, the specific discipline and the errors commonly encountered when working across languages isn't able to make sense of what you're trying to say, it's very difficult to provide assistance. When we read papers for our clients, we strike up a dialogue in marginal comments, and this is a good way for clients to start a dialogue with us as well. So if you're having trouble with a particular construction or a specific section in your paper, explain the problem as well as you can in a comment. If you're translating a quoted passage, let us know it's your translation and we'll check the English and improve it if necessary. This sort of proactive approach will help us direct attention where it is most needed and help you maximise the effect of the money you spend on professional proofreading.

PART II: PREPARING, PRESENTING AND POLISHING
YOUR WORK

CHAPTER 5
Presenting Data and Sources Accurately and Effectively

Journal guidelines vary greatly when it comes to the advice they provide about presenting data and referring to sources. In some cases separate sections containing detailed instructions about exactly how to lay out tables and figures and how to format citations and references will be provided, while in others authors will simply be advised to format tables and figures in 'an appropriate' manner and will be lucky to find two or three reference examples to follow. Tables and figures do seem to receive fairly good coverage in the guidelines of most scholarly journals, however, and generally you will be able to find some indication of the referencing style required. So read anything and everything you can find in the guidelines about these elements of your paper, pay careful attention to any models provided (both appropriate and inappropriate), consult any manuals or other style guides mentioned and take a close look at papers already published by the journal to see how references, tables and figures were successfully formatted. What you learn can be both followed and used to inspire your own designs when constructing your references, tables and figures.

5.1   Tables, Figures and Other Research Data: Guidelines and Good Practice

Although the advice I share in this section should not be taken as a substitute for journal guidelines when it comes to the layout of tables and figures, it stems from a familiarity with the guidelines of many journals and the experience of encountering many tables and figures that present unfamiliar data. As with every other aspect of your paper, clarity, accuracy and precision are essential, and in the case of tables and figures, there's little space for explanation, so data must for the most part stand on their own, with only the format you shape around them to lend structure and meaning. This means that the format of your tables and figures needs to be thought out very carefully: there needs to be enough space both to present and to separate all the information your tables and figures contain in ways that facilitate your readers' understanding. Poorly laid out tables and figures can instead obscure that understanding, so it's important to analyse your tables and figures as a reader would, seeking the information you're providing, and then edit and reshape until your tables and figures achieve just what they should. Some journals will insist that tables and figures only be used if they include or illustrate information not presented elsewhere in the paper, and frown on those that repeat data in any way. So the first consideration should be whether you need tables and figures to share your research and results effectively and, if so, what exactly those tables and figures should contain. Illustrating devices or conditions discussed in a paper, providing graphs and lists of data that cannot be accommodated in detail in an article and highlighting the most significant aspects of the results of a study are a few of many reasons to provide tables and figures for your readers.

Once you've decided that your paper does require tables and/or figures, some basic practices and concerns found in the guidelines of many journals should be considered. For tables, for instance, ask yourself if you will you require lines or rules to separate the material – some journals ask that vertical lines be avoided, others that rules of all kinds be avoided, and a table may take more space on the page if you need to construct it without lines. For figures, there is the matter of using colour or not: some journals only print tables in monochrome (black and white) and include figures in colour solely online, while others will be happy to print your figures in colour, but they may charge a significant amount for it, so you'll need to decide whether printing the figures in colour is worth the cost. For both tables and figures, consider the overall size of each item in terms of the printed page of the journal, and if your tables or figures will need to be reduced to such a degree that they may no longer be clear or legible, you may have to present the information in a different format or divide the information you've compiled in one table or figure into two or three tables or figures. Online publication is often the best route for large tables and figures, and colour rarely proves a problem with online publication.

Remember as you're constructing your tables and figures that as a general rule each table and figure should be able to stand alone, whether it's printed amidst the text of your paper or published separately online. For this reason, all abbreviations beyond the standard ones for common measures (cm, Hz, mph, N, SD, etc.) will need to be defined either in the table or figure itself or in close association with it, and this is the case even if you've already defined the abbreviations in your paper and in any preceding tables or figures. You can choose to write each term out in full within the body of the table or figure, or introduce and define the abbreviations in the heading or title of a table or in the caption or legend of a figure, or you can define any abbreviations used in a note at the bottom of the table or figure. This last approach is used for tables more often than for figures, and the abbreviations within a table are usually connected to the definitions in the note via superscript lowercase letters (but not always, so do check the journal guidelines). If you're in any doubt about whether an abbreviation should be defined for your readers, it's best to define it: such attention is a sign of conscientious documentation, and if the journal deems the definition unnecessary, it can always be removed.

Be sure that the terms you use in your tables and figures match those you use in the paper itself precisely, and that the abbreviations take the same forms in both the paper and the tables and figures. In fact, it's essential to ensure that all the data presented in tables and figures are entirely consistent with data presented in the paper (and the abstract as well). This is to say that the format in which you present similar data in both places should be identical, and any overlapping data should be exactly the same in content as well as format in both places. Remember that data stand alone in a table or figure, so they need to be perfect and should be checked more than once by more than one pair of knowledgeable eyes. Even a simple error can not only render the information incorrect, it can also alter the overall appearance of the table or figure, and since an effective visual representation of information is precisely the goal of tables and figures, this can be disastrous. All numbers in a table or figure can be written as numerals and should be accurately formatted in keeping with English convention and/or journal guidelines (on the use of numbers in academic or scientific prose, see Section 4.4.1 above).

Journal guidelines should also be consulted to determine exactly how to place and submit your tables and figures in relation to your paper. Variations are myriad: when submitting to some journals you can simply place your tables and figures where you'd have them located in the published version; others will want all tables and figures added at the end of the document and only placement notes – e.g., 'Insert Table 1 here' and 'Figure 3 about here' – within the body of the paper. 'Added at the end of the document' can mean either before or after the reference list, and for some journals tables should precede figures, whereas for others it's just the opposite. Sometimes guidelines will ask that tables be embedded in or tacked onto the end of the paper, but the figures submitted in separate files, with only the figure legends included in the paper, usually at the end. The point is to note and comply with whatever is required: it's disappointing to discover that guidelines won't let you use tables and figures quite as you'd hoped, but better that than writing the paper with the tables and figures you want only to have it rejected because of them or (in the best scenario) have to rewrite your paper completely with different, fewer or no tables at all. If a set number or style or size of tables and figures is absolutely central to your paper, then be sure to choose a journal that allows it.

However many or few tables and figures you use, be sure to label each one accurately and to refer to each of them in the body of your paper as you report and discuss your results. Virtually all journal guidelines specify this (and others expect it), and it's also a simple courtesy to your reader that facilitates that reader's understanding of your paper and your tables and figures in relation to it. Unnumbered or misnumbered figures and tables to which the reader is not accurately and precisely referred at an appropriate point in the text defeat their own purpose and negate some of the hard work that went into making them by leaving it to the reader to sort out the relationship between your text and your tables and figures. Tables and figures should also be referred to in numerical order, which means that they should be numbered according to the order in which they are mentioned in the text regardless of where they are actually placed in relation to the text. For clarity, they should also be referred to by number whenever mentioned, with the usual format being 'Figure 1' or 'Table 2,' unless, of course, the journal guidelines specify a different format (such as 'Fig.1'), and whatever format used to refer to a table or figure should match that used in the heading or caption to label the table or figure itself. In the heading/caption for a table or figure, a full stop usually follows the number (Table 1. Demographic characteristics of study participants) unless there are instructions in the guidelines to the contrary (calling for a colon, for instance, after the number instead of a full stop). The title or heading of a table is generally placed above the table, whereas figure captions or legends often appear beneath figures, but guidelines (as well as style manuals) differ on this as well, so again, reading and following the guidelines of the specific journal is essential to success (see also Section 1.2 above).

Finally, if you are using in your figures any images for which the copyright belongs to someone other than yourself, you'll need to acknowledge the source(s), usually in the relevant figure captions, and you'll also need to obtain permissions to reproduce such images. Although all permissions need not be obtained until your paper is accepted for publication in a journal, it's a good idea to indicate when you submit your paper which figures will require permissions and from which individuals and institutions those permissions will need to be requested, as well as noting any permissions that you've already obtained. Planning ahead when it comes to permissions can prevent delays and help speed up the publication process, but remember, too, that permissions to reproduce images from other publications can be costly and the expense is usually met by the author, so it's a good idea to consider carefully whether reproducing images and other material that require permissions is really necessary and worth the cost.

PRS Tip:

So much attention is paid to numerical data in tables and images in figures that the words appearing in tables and figures sometimes suffer neglect. If the words used in tables and figures do not effectively clarify and categorise the information presented, the reader's understanding suffers as well. So when using words in a table or figure, it's good to keep these basic practices in mind:

- *Use standard abbreviations for measures and define all abbreviations beyond those for common measures.*
- *Use terms and abbreviations that match exactly those used for the same concepts, categories and measures in the paper and in its other tables and figures.*
- *Make sure that all words are visible and legible, and not obscured or crowded by other elements of the table or figure.*
- *Do not allow a word to be split inappropriately onto two separate lines – use a wider column instead.*
- *Use capitalisation consistently throughout the tables and figures in a paper.*
- *If the table or figure was originally prepared in another language, translate all words into accurate English – if you're writing for an English-speaking audience, all aspects of your paper, including your tables and figures, should be entirely legible to that audience.*

5.2 Last but Not Least: References, Citations and Quotations

Some of you are no doubt already shuddering, and accurate referencing can be a challenge, but it need not be a nightmare. It does require a significant investment of both time and careful attention, however, and the research in a paper, like the argument, is the author's own, so you are the only one who can truly judge when a citation of any given source is appropriate. In many cases you are also the only one among your first readers (including proofreaders, student assistants, colleagues and that all-important journal editor) who has access to the complete bibliographical information for your references. It is your responsibility as an academic or scientific author to record your references with absolute integrity and precision, and getting them right is well worth the effort, not only because sound references are a quality of sound scholarship, but also because the consequences can be unpleasant for both the author and the journal if the bibliographical details in a paper, and worse yet the intellectual use of sources, are misrepresented or simply wrong.

So you should begin by recording your sources and every aspect of the use you make of them accurately and thoroughly. This is a process best achieved by keeping detailed, accurate and up-to-date records during the design, research and trial stages of your study. Such records will give you the raw material you need to build your reference list and effectively connect your in-text citations to the sources the list includes. Journal guidelines should then be read with extreme care, paying close attention to all examples provided to determine exactly what style of referencing you should use. Any manuals or style guides recommended by the guidelines should also be consulted, especially if you find yourself dealing with an unusual source or one for which you can find in the journal guidelines neither an example nor precise instructions as to how to record it. Finally, you will need to do your best to provide all the information necessary in the correct order, format and position, and check it all with the utmost care (and ideally more than once with more than one set of eyes) for accuracy and consistency of spelling, dates, quotations, capitalisation, punctuation, fonts, abbreviations and so on.

So yes, good referencing takes a lot of work, but if you're lucky enough to have a capable graduate student who could use a little extra cash, helping you sort out the details of your references and citations can be an excellent way for a student to learn about the nitty-gritty of publishing in an academic or scientific journal. The final responsibility lies with the author, however, and the sections below suggest some practices and methods that may prove helpful.

5.2.1 In-Text Citations and Quotations:
Where and How To Acknowledge Sources

Although referencing styles vary considerably among style manuals and journal guidelines, and any required variations should always be followed to the letter, there are three basic methods of referring to sources in the body of an academic or scientific paper: author-date citations (which tend to be used in the physical, natural and social sciences, although the Modern Language Association style sometimes used in the humanities varies this slightly by not using a date), numerical citations (frequently the referencing choice for papers in the medical and biological sciences) and citations contained in either footnotes or endnotes (preferred by many scholars working in the humanities). The first two methods are discussed in this section and the third in Section 5.2.2 below.

In all three cases, the basic principle of when to provide a reference or citation remains the same: whenever you use the ideas or methods or results or words of another author, you should provide a reference to that author's work, but exactly where to place the citation varies. If, for instance, you're discussing an author's work or using his or her ideas throughout a sentence, then the end of the sentence is usually the best place for the reference. If you're making use of a source throughout a whole paragraph, then be sure to provide the reference with the sentence in which you first begin referring to the source, rather than waiting until the end of the paragraph, although it's fine to include a citation at the end of the paragraph as well, and good, too, to include a citation whenever you feel it might be appropriate to acknowledge the author again in the midst of the paragraph. Certainly if you're referring to more than one source by the same author, you should provide a reference to each source wherever relevant. If only part of a sentence makes use of a particular source, then the citation to that source should come immediately after the relevant material in the sentence so that it's clear exactly what part of your work is dependent on that source. If part of the sentence makes use of one source and the next part borrows from another source, then provide two citations, with the appropriate source cited after the relevant information in each case. You can also provide these two citations (or more if necessary) together at the end of the sentence: although this is most appropriate if the sentence as a whole makes use of both sources, a few guidelines call for all citations to be clustered at the end of sentences or paragraphs. Generally speaking, however, when you quote an author directly, it's essential that you provide a citation at once, and include with it the number of the page on which the words you've quoted can be found.

In an author-date system of referencing, the last name (or names) of the author (or authors) should be provided along with the publication date of the source. This can be done entirely in parentheses – 'The study (Smith, 2010) showed...' – or by mentioning the author's name in the main text and including the date in parentheses: 'Smith's study (2010) showed....' If you provide two or more references to works by the same author within a single set of parentheses (or square brackets if the guidelines call for them instead), the dates should be arranged chronologically and separated by commas – (Smith, 2010, 2012, 2013) or more rarely the other way around (Smith, 2013, 2012, 2010) but not (Smith, 2012, 2010, 2013) – and the order used in the in-text citations should match that used in the reference list (see Section 5.2.3). If references to different authors are provided within a single set of parentheses, then the citations should be separated by semi-colons and arranged either alphabetically by author name (matching their order in the reference list) or chronologically by date or using a combination of both, depending on the referencing style. In APA style, for instance, this would be the correct format: (Jones, 2013; McGraw, 2003; McGraw & Hill, 2001; Smith, 2010, 2012). Chicago referencing, on the other hand, leaves the order up to the author, whether alphabetical or chronological, but whichever order is used in whichever style, specific journal guidelines should be accommodated and the pattern decided upon should be used consistently throughout the paper.

There are various other differences between individual referencing styles. Some use a comma between the author's name and the date as I have in the preceding paragraph (Smith, 2010) and some do not (Smith 2010). Some use an ampersand (&) while others use 'and' between author names for sources with more than one author, but as a general rule, 'and' should be used in the main text – 'McGraw and Hill (2003) argue that...' – even if an ampersand is used parenthetically (McGraw & Hill, 2003). The use of 'et al.' in in-text citations also varies from style to style: in Chicago and Harvard referencing, for instance, 'et al.' should be used after the first author's name if the source has four or more authors, though Harvard style also allows the use of 'et al.' when a source has only three authors. Chicago style uses a full stop after 'et al.' (Thompson et al. 2008), whereas Harvard referencing does not (Thompson et al, 2008). Sometimes 'et al.' should appear in italic font, but this is usually a requirement of specific journals. In APA style, 'et al.' is followed by a full stop and italics are not required, but when to use 'et al.' is a little more complicated. If a source has three to five authors, all authors should be listed for the first citation in a paper (Thompson, Smith, Jones, & Johnson, 2008), but all subsequent in-text references should use the first author's name followed by 'et al.' (Thompson et al., 2008), so special care needs to be taken to ensure that each citation appears in the correct format. For six or more authors, APA style uses 'et al.' after the first author's name in all references to the source, including the first one (on the use of 'et al.,' see also Section 4.2).

If you find that you use in your paper two or more sources with the same date and by the same author (or authors), you'll need to add a lowercase letter to each date regardless of which author-date referencing system you're using (Smith, 2010a, 2010b; Thompson et al., 2008a). You will need to add these letters to the dates of the same sources in your reference list as well so that your in-text references successfully lead your readers to the right source in every case. In fact, everything about the author and date information provided in in-text citations within a paper must correspond exactly to the same information in the accompanying reference list, so author names and dates should be carefully compared between the paper and list to ensure absolute accuracy. Finally, your parenthetical citations should also be appropriately positioned in relation to the punctuation of your sentences, generally before any punctuation marks: e.g., 'According to Smith (2010a), there was...' and '...just as a recent study has shown (Smith, 2012).'

In a numerical system of referencing such as that required by Vancouver style and the guidelines of a number of journals that call for variations on the Vancouver system, each source used is assigned an Arabic (rarely a Roman) numeral and that same number is used every time the same source is cited in a paper. The sources are numbered according to the order in which they are referred to in the paper, so the first source cited will be number 1, the second, number 2, and so on. The method for numbering any references that appear in tables and figures differs between guidelines: some would have such references numbered after all those in the paper itself, while others ask that references in a table or figure be numbered according to where the table or figure is mentioned in the paper. It's essential to number sources correctly because errors can mean having to change the numbers of all sources cited after a misnumbered one in both the paper and the reference list. Using numbers for citations doesn't mean that author names and dates cannot be provided if you want or need this information in your paper, but only that they don't need to be and that a source's number must appear in the text whether you provide additional information or not: 'In 2003, McGraw and Hill studied this phenomenon.(1)' Vancouver style sets the reference numbers inside parentheses or what it calls 'round brackets' (as I've done in the example above) or uses a superscript font for them: 'McGraw and Hill[1] argue that....' However, some journal guidelines will call for square brackets instead [1].

Groups of citations can be gathered together in a numerical referencing style much as they are in an author-date system simply by listing the numbers of all relevant sources separated by commas (1,2,5,8,12). If three or more consecutive numbers need to be listed, a hyphen should be used between the first and last numbers (1-3,5-9). In Vancouver referencing, no spaces are used between the numbers, but some journals will provide examples that do use spaces, so be sure to check the journal guidelines for precise instructions. As with an author-date referencing style, Vancouver-style citations should be appropriately positioned to indicate with accuracy your use of sources in your text, but standard placement in relation to punctuation calls for the reference numbers to follow full stops and commas ('According to McGraw and Hill,[1] ...') and precede colons and semi-colons ('The following categories are considered in McGraw and Hill[1]: ...'). Again, however, journal guidelines sometimes call for slightly different placement (before commas and full stops, for example), so always check those guidelines.

Whether you're using an author-date or a numerical referencing style for your in-text citations, you will need to provide a page number (or page numbers) when you quote directly from a source. The format for recording page numbers varies from style to style:

- APA: (Smith, 2010, p. 222) and for multiple pages (Smith, 2010, pp. 222-223)
- Chicago: (Smith 2010, 222) and for multiple pages (Smith 2010, 222–223)
- Harvard: (Smith, 2010:p.222) and for multiple pages (Smith, 2010:pp.222-223)
- Vancouver in parentheses or square brackets: Smith (1 p222) and for multiple pages Smith [1 pp222-223]
- Vancouver in superscript font: Smith[1(p222)] and for multiple pages Smith[1(pp222-223)]
- MLA (Modern Language Association), which cites page numbers even when there is no direct quotation: (Smith 222) and for multiple pages (Smith 222-223)

Notice that the punctuation between page numbers is usually a hyphen, but sometimes (in the case of Chicago referencing above, for instance, and also in the reference examples provided by some journals) a longer dash is used: either way, there should be no space on either side of the hyphen or dash. Beyond that, spacing varies between styles, and so does the use of a full stop after p. or pp. Page ranges can be condensed in format (pp.222-23 or pp.222-3 instead of pp.222-223), but only if the guidelines you're following clearly indicate that this is permitted; if in doubt or deciding for yourself, use the full number on both sides of the hyphen or dash. If the source you're quoting does not have page numbers (many online sources, for instance, do not), try to be as precise as possible about the location of the words you quote so your reader can find the passage: (Smith, 2007, Discussion section, para. 4) is a good APA example. However, some styles and guidelines will ask that authors do not provide paragraph numbers unless the paragraphs are already numbered in the source.

It was once the case that double quotation marks (" ") were seen as more American and single ones (' ') as more British, but both kinds are used for direct quotation in both forms of English now. Many journal guidelines and some style manuals will have little or nothing to say on the matter, but the quotation examples they provide will sometimes help you determine which type of marks to use: both APA and Vancouver styles, for instance, show examples using double quotation marks. Articles already published by a journal will also provide examples to consult, but you will often find that one paper uses one kind and one another. This means that either is acceptable to the journal, so you will need to choose which to use, with the key being to use the same type of quotation marks whenever you are quoting a source directly. It is also a good idea to use the other type of quotation marks when you are not quoting but using quotation marks only to emphasise words and phrases: double quotation marks for direct quotations, for example, and single ones for emphasis (or vice versa). In this way, you make it clear to your readers exactly when you are quoting from a source and when you are not. In this guide, for instance, letters, words, phrases and longer examples of the forms I'm discussing are enclosed in single quotation marks ('emphasis'), but direct quotations from other sources are enclosed in double quotation marks ("quotation").

Emphasis on terms and phrases can also be achieved through the use of italic font, and some journal guidelines express preferences in this regard, but italics should not be used as an indication of quotation: that is, every quoted word need not be in italics. Italics should only be used in quotations for two specific reasons: for one, they are used if italic font is already on certain words in the quotation (for emphasis perhaps, or on foreign vocabulary), in which case including them on the same words is simply quoting accurately. Sometimes, especially in informal publications (theses and dissertations, for example), underlining (or underscoring) will appear instead of italics: since this is simply a form of emphasis used when the italic font is not available, underlining can be represented in quotation by either underlining or italics. Italics can also be used in quotations if you wish to add your own emphasis to some of the quoted words, but if you choose to do this, you need to acknowledge the italics as your own: Smith explains that his 'results did *not* reveal the trend of rapid deterioration noted in previous studies' (2010, p. 222; italics my own).

Punctuation practices with regard to quotations differ among styles and guidelines, with some systems, for instance, placing the full stop or comma associated with your own sentence within the closing quotation mark ('...noted in previous studies.') and others placing it outside ('...noted in previous studies'.). In this *Guide* I've set full stops and commas inside quotation marks. If a parenthetical reference follows a quotation, the closing punctuation should always come after the reference. Colons, semi-colons, question marks and exclamations should be added after the closing quotation mark unless they are present in the source you're quoting, in which case they should be included within the quotation. Minor changes in punctuation and capitalisation can be made to a quotation if the changes are necessary to make the quotation work effectively within the grammar and structure of your own sentence. So, for example, if you're quoting a whole sentence, you can change the initial capital to a lowercase letter: According to Smith (2010), 'the results did not reveal the trend of rapid deterioration noted in previous studies' (p. 222, where the first 'The' bore an uppercase 'T' in the original). These minor changes do not require the use of square brackets.

Beyond minor changes in punctuation and capitalisation in quotations, any quoted material should be provided in your paper in the exact same format as it appears in the source. When you need to add something significant to a quoted passage to make it work in your own sentence, you should use square brackets around the added material: Smith (2010, p. 222) was surprised that his 'results did not reveal the trend of rapid deterioration [because this trend had been] noted in previous studies.' An ellipsis, on the other hand, should be used when you delete words from the middle of a quotation: Smith (2010, p. 222) was surprised that his 'results did not reveal the trend...noted in previous studies.' An ellipsis is not required, however, at the beginning or end of a quotation (I use ellipses in those positions in some examples, not quotations, in this *Guide* simply to clarify relevant formats). It is always best to change as little as possible in a quotation; after all, you're presumably quoting the words of another author because they serve your present purpose. Long quotations (40 words or more is a common guideline) are best indented as block quotations: these start on a new line, are noticeably indented on the left-hand side, and do not require quotation marks.

All quotations should be introduced and discussed clearly and accurately. Beyond the formatting techniques above which will let your readers know that a quotation is a quotation, identifying the author (or speaker) is often helpful and the quoted material should definitely be logically connected to the argument of your paper. With the exception of quotations that contain pithy, proverbial sayings that neatly sum up concepts, or passages addressing the very issues with which you are dealing in the same or similar language, quotations aren't really able to move an argument on their own: they can do a lot, but they need to be used thoughtfully and their function in your paper should always be clear. Your readers may not be making the same connections you are, so those connections need to be explained. Always use a quotation in a way that makes it absolutely clear exactly how it relates to your present argument, perhaps analyse it in some detail in relation to your own thoughts or evidence, and definitely explain any terminology or concepts used in it if you do not use (and explain) the same language and terminology in your own text. An author quotes to make his or her evidence and arguments more interesting, more striking and more persuasive, but a quotation cannot achieve this if you do not explain for your readers your thoughts about a quoted passage and how both it and those thoughts fit into your argument.

5.2.2 Footnotes and Endnotes: Do You Need Them?

Footnotes or endnotes – sometimes both in combination – were once staples of a scholarly paper, but they play a much smaller part in academic and scientific papers today, and many journals will ask that they be kept to a minimum or avoided altogether. Those journals that do allow notes will usually specify which they prefer – footnotes at the bottom of the pages or endnotes at the end of the document – and many will ask that either kind of notes be restricted to additional information and not used for referencing. This is because many journals now use author-date or numerical referencing styles, and referencing via footnotes or endnotes is a different style altogether, one almost exclusively restricted to the humanities (likely because of its capacity for accommodating a wide variety of sources) that tends to be used in books more than in journals.

When you're using an author-date or numerical in-text referencing style, footnotes and endnotes should not be used exclusively for referencing or for providing full bibliographical information about sources. This does not mean, however, that you can't use citations in your notes: on the contrary, you should treat notes just like any other part of your text, writing and punctuating them as full sentences and providing the same kind of short references you use in your text (see the footnote here for an example).[2] Your notes have to do more than simply provide references, however; they have to add information such as details, alternative approaches, additional evidence and the like to the main discussion.

When you're using an in-note style of referencing, on the other hand, footnotes and endnotes can exist for no other reason than to provide

---

[2] The most interesting aspect of Smith's research from my perspective is that his 'results did not reveal the trend of rapid deterioration noted in previous studies' (2010, p. 222).

references. In this referencing system the notes generally provide complete bibliographical information when a source is first cited (as footnotes 1, 5 & 6 in this *Guide* do: see Sections 4.3, 6.2.1 & 7.3.3) and a shorter version of the reference (usually the author's last name and a shortened title) for all subsequent citations of the same source. Using the Chicago style of referencing within notes as an example, the citations would appear in this format:

- Full footnote/endnote reference with page number: Kathryn Kerby-Fulton, Maidie Hilmo and Linda Olson, *Opening Up Middle English Manuscripts: Literary and Visual Approaches* (Ithaca, NY: Cornell University Press, 2012), 318.
- Subsequent footnote/endnote reference with page number: Kerby-Fulton, Hilmo and Olson, *Opening Up Middle English Manuscripts*, 318.

With this style of referencing, a reference list isn't strictly necessary because all the bibliographical information required to find sources has already been provided in the notes, but a bibliography is sometimes included (see Section 5.2.3).

Although the primary function of footnotes or endnotes in an in-note referencing style is to provide citations and bibliographical information on sources, additional material of all kinds can also be included in the notes, making them a useful site for comparing and contrasting theories and evidence and results, and creating a kind of secondary dialogue within the discussion of a paper. However, many publishers now view such notes as clutter on the page and often relegate them as endnotes to the end of an article or chapter or book in order to avoid what is seen as an unattractive problem. Unfortunately, notes tend to be read less often when they appear at the end of a document rather than as footnotes on each page, so this fact should be considered when deciding whether to include notes in your paper or not, regardless of which referencing system you're using. Check the journal guidelines, comply with any requirements and as a general rule for modern publication, use notes as little as possible – that is, only when you need to do so.

When you do use notes, remember that they should be written in full sentences and correctly punctuated – footnotes and endnotes are not the place for point-form information or English that is informal or shorthand. Note numbers generally take the form of superscript Arabic numerals (as I've used for the footnotes in this *Guide*; only very rarely are Roman numerals used) placed where they are most relevant in the text, but some journals ask that note numbers be enclosed in square brackets [1] or parentheses (1). Like numerical references, they usually follow full stops and commas,[3] and precede colons and semi-colons[4]; however, most journals that allow notes will provide some guidance on how to use them, so always consult and follow the guidelines. The font used in footnotes and endnotes should be the same as the font used in the main paper (although the automatic note function in a program such as Word will often use a different one, so do watch for this and adjust the font if necessary), but the text in notes can be a little smaller than the text in the main document (a 10-point instead of 12-point font, for instance), so long as the text remains clear and legible in relation to the size of the main text and complies with any font size requirements provided by the journal.

5.2.3   Reference Lists and Bibliographies: Niggling Details

Compiling and recording sources in a reference list (or list of works cited in MLA style) or bibliography is more than simply attending to niggling details, of course – it's a big job and constitutes a significant part of an academic or scientific paper – but the process can certainly give an author the impression of drowning in niggling details. As soon as the rules of any particular referencing style or set of guidelines begin to sink in, allowing the beleaguered compiler to surface for air, an exception pops up, and there are always exceptions – sources of a kind that just isn't mentioned in the guidelines you're using or unique sources that seem to belong in more than one of the reference categories you're trying to follow or simply don't fit any of the rules provided. So compiling a perfect list of sources, whether you call it References or Works Cited or Bibliography, can be a

---

[3] This example shows how to place a footnote number in relation to a comma or full stop.
[4] This example shows how to place a footnote number in relation to a semi-colon or colon.

challenge as much of patience as precision, and as dull a task as many find it, a touch of imagination never hurts as you wrestle the many multimedia resources that tend to inform today's academic and scientific articles into what remains a very traditional form of acknowledging and sharing scholarly sources. Being both accurate and thorough is as important today as it was 100 years ago – without all the correct information accurately recorded, you neither adequately nor respectfully acknowledge the work of other scholars, and you also make it difficult for your readers to find your sources. Today, the effect of a reference list, for good or ill, is immediate: your paper and sources appear online in many cases before they ever see print, and immediately enter a complex web of cross references on which scholars rely for a variety of reasons, from reviews of literature to assessments of journals.

Referencing styles and guidelines differ so markedly at times and in such tiny details at others that general advice beyond a mantra chanting 'precision, precision, precision, consistency, consistency, consistency' in your ear can only be so helpful. There are some general trends and distinctions that are worth knowing, however: a bibliography, for instance, is usually arranged alphabetically by the last names of authors (for help with the details of alphabetical order, most style manuals – the *APA Manual* is a good example – will provide instructions and examples), and a bibliography can contain not just all the sources you actually cite in your paper, but also any sources that you don't directly cite in your paper but that nonetheless influenced your thinking as you did your research and drafted your article. A list of references or works cited, on the other hand, includes only the sources – all of them – that you cite in your paper. If you're using an author-date style of citation, your reference list will be arranged alphabetically by authors' last names just as a bibliography is, but while a bibliography usually includes the publication date near the end of a reference, in an author-date system the date of a source will follow immediately after the author name(s) in the list because dates are part of the way in which readers will find and identify sources. Dates should be kept in mind while listing references in both systems, however, since they determine the order in which sources by the same author(s) should be listed: some systems arrange such items with the earliest publication first moving forward in time to the latest, while others will have you list the most recent publication first with others following in reverse chronological order. For numerical referencing styles, neither author names nor dates are used to arrange the sources; instead, items are listed in the reference list in numerical order (the same order in which they're cited in the paper) because in this case it is the number of a source that allows your readers to find and identify it.

The spacing and indentation of bibliographies and reference lists vary considerably as well. The relevant style manual or journal guidelines will provide details, but as a general rule maintaining the line spacing (double, for instance) you've used in the paper itself is a good policy, and using indentation and/or spacing to separate your references clearly and improve their legibility is good practice. A number of standard abbreviations are used in reference lists and bibliographies – 'pp.,' 'Ed.,' 'ed.,' 'edn.,' 'Vol.,' 'No.' and the two-letter abbreviations for American states are common examples – but these, too, vary between referencing styles, and some journals will encourage the use of further abbreviations, such as the standard abbreviations for journal titles (which can be found in various places online: the NLM Catalog of Journals Referenced in the NCBI Databases is an easy-to-use example). The bibliographical information in reference lists and bibliographies also differs between styles in the format of page number ranges (e.g., 222-4 vs. 222-24 vs. 222-224), and in the use of punctuation, capitalisation and fonts (on journal volume numbers, for instance, APA style uses italic font, whereas the guidelines for the medical journal *BMC Public Health* call for bold font on volume numbers).

As a tool to help you take careful note of the many elements that vary from style to style, I'm providing here a list of the same source (a chapter within an edited book) recorded in the bibliography/references/works cited formats required by eight different styles:

- Chicago Bibliography (in-note): Hardman, Phillipa. "Presenting the Text: Pictorial Tradition in Fifteenth-Century Manuscripts of the *Canterbury Tales*." In *Chaucer Illustrated: Five Hundred Years of the Canterbury Tales in Pictures*, edited by William K. Finley and Joseph Rosenblum, 37–72. New Castle, DE: Oak Knoll Press, 2003.
- MLA (author-page or author-short title-page if necessary): Hardman, Phillipa. "Presenting the Text: Pictorial Tradition in Fifteenth-Century Manuscripts of the *Canterbury Tales*." *Chaucer Illustrated: Five Hundred Years of the Canterbury Tales in Pictures*. Ed. William K. Finley and Joseph Rosenblum. New Castle, DE: Oak Knoll Press, 2003. 37-72. Print.
- Vancouver (numerical): 1. Hardman P. Presenting the text: pictorial tradition in fifteenth-century manuscripts of the *Canterbury Tales*. In: Finley WK, Rosenblum J, editors. Chaucer illustrated: Five hundred years of the *Canterbury Tales* in pictures. New Castle (DE): Oak Knoll Press; 2003. Pp. 37-72.
- American Medical Association (AMA: numerical): 1. Hardman P. Presenting the text: pictorial tradition in fifteenth-century manuscripts of the *Canterbury Tales*. In: Finley WK, Rosenblum J, eds. *Chaucer Illustrated: Five Hundred Years of the Canterbury Tales in Pictures*. New Castle, De: Oak Knoll Press; 2003:37-72.
- BMC Public Health (numerical): 1. Hardman P: **Presenting the text: pictorial tradition in fifteenth-century manuscripts of the *Canterbury Tales***. In *Chaucer Illustrated: Five Hundred Years of the Canterbury Tales in Pictures*. Edited by Finley WK, Rosenblum J. New Castle, DE: Oak Knoll Press; 2003:37-72.
- APA (author-date): Hardman, P. (2003). Presenting the text: Pictorial tradition in fifteenth-century manuscripts of the *Canterbury Tales*. In W. K. Finley & J. Rosenblum (Eds.), *Chaucer illustrated: Five hundred years of the Canterbury Tales in pictures* (pp. 37-72). New Castle, DE: Oak Knoll Press.
- Chicago Reference List (author-date): Hardman, Phillipa. 2003. "Presenting the Text: Pictorial Tradition in Fifteenth-Century Manuscripts of the *Canterbury Tales*." In *Chaucer Illustrated: Five Hundred Years of the Canterbury Tales in Pictures*, edited by William K. Finley and Joseph Rosenblum, 37–72. New Castle, DE: Oak Knoll Press.

- Harvard (author-date): Hardman, P. (2003) Presenting the text: Pictorial tradition in fifteenth-century manuscripts of the *Canterbury Tales*. In: Finley, W. K. & Rosenblum, J. (eds.) *Chaucer Illustrated: Five Hundred Years of the Canterbury Tales in Pictures*. New Castle, DE, Oak Knoll Press, pp.37-72.

A close examination of these examples reveals not only many of the differences in formatting and arrangement used by a selection of common styles, but also, and equally importantly, the consistency with which all eight styles record the same details about the source despite the variations (with MLA style calling for the medium of publication – print in this case – as well). It is essential that you provide complete bibliographical information of this sort for each and every source in your list, so a careful check through all your references is necessary once they're typed in. You should also double-check each reference against the original for accuracy, against others like it for consistency, and against the citations of it in your paper to be sure that names, dates, reference numbers and any other information that appear in both places are identical. If you use any sources in languages other than English, you may want to translate the titles into English in your reference list or bibliography (some journals will insist on this): a standard way to do this is to place the English translation in square brackets immediately after the original title. Remember to provide URLs and DOIs (uniform resource locators and digital object identifiers) for sources that you accessed online, and, if the style or guidelines you're using require it, an access or retrieval date. Finally, be sure to check the journal guidelines regarding the number of references you are allowed to use in your paper: some journals will set a limit of 20 or 40 references, for instance, depending on the type of paper.

PRS Tip:
Even when all instructions are followed and the utmost care is taken to cite sources accurately and construct a thorough reference list or bibliography, errors and inconsistencies will inevitably creep in, and correcting them is especially time-consuming because each and every detail needs to be checked against both the sources and the style sheet or guidelines. A professional proofreader familiar with academic and scientific referencing styles can be of enormous assistance, but a proofreader cannot provide citations or construct a reference list for you. So the key to making a proofreader's work serve you well is to do your very best to provide appropriate citations in your text and complete bibliographical information in your list in as consistent a manner as possible that conforms as closely as you can manage to the style with which you're working. Then send your paper and your reference list, along with information about the style or guidelines you're following, to us at PRS, and we'll check, correct and comment on these aspects of your work. If you're using your own format for references, be especially careful to be as consistent as possible throughout your list, because only if you set the pattern clearly can a proofreader determine what that pattern is and help you conform to it as he or she ensures that all your references are complete and adhere to good academic or scientific practice.

5.3   Automatic Formatting: To Use or Not To Use

The various kinds of automatic formatting available in software programs such as Word and Endnote can be incredibly helpful: they will manage and arrange many aspects of an academic or scientific paper, including spacing and indentation, lists of different kinds, numbered headings, footnotes and endnotes, tables and charts, and citations and reference lists. However, they need to be used with care and only if the journal guidelines you're working with allow such automatic formatting. Some journals discourage authors from using automatic referencing of any kind, for instance, asking that citations and reference lists be compiled (typed in) manually, while others encourage the use of automatic referencing, and the same variation in requirements occurs with regard to tables, notes and even indentation. So the guidelines should always be consulted and every effort should be made to comply with them, particularly by not using any sort of formatting the guidelines bother to mention as undesirable.

When in doubt, however, or when left to your own devices in the absence of specific instructions, it's usually best to avoid automatic formatting, particularly the more complicated kinds, as much as possible. As a general rule, too much formatting can cause problems for publishers and much of the formatting that authors add to their papers is simply removed by some journals during copyediting. In the worst case scenario, a paper will be rejected or returned for revision when too much unwanted formatting (double columns, for instance, or tables formatted by the wrong program) is present. Yet it's also important that you lay out your article in such a way that the editor can readily see how you intend your paper to look, and making your paper look good is, of course, a large part of the reason behind all the details I've provided above about presentation, so the use of automatic formatting is another instance of the need to find and maintain a delicate balance.

You also need to proofread with great care any part of your paper that you've constructed through automatic formatting. Never assume that the program has 'got it all right' because this is all too rarely the case. Check every word, every number and every bit of punctuation; pay attention to font styles and sizes and patterns of capitalisation. Automatic referencing, for instance, may achieve a format very close to the style you need, but one particular detail will consistently be wrong, or unusual or complicated references will be formatted in inappropriate ways. So each reference will need to be checked and, if necessary, corrected manually. Automatic numbering of lists and sections usually comes out accurately, but sometimes an item or heading is typed or pasted into a document in such a way that the program doesn't recognise that it needs to be numbered, and while this may be simple enough to remedy in a list of six items, when misnumbering occurs in the sections of a paper that contains many subsections and cross references based on that incorrect numbering, the problem can quickly increase in magnitude and take considerable time and attention to repair. So if you let your word processing program number your sections, watch what it's doing as you write and correct any errors immediately before they grow into larger problems.

On the whole, automatic formatting is a useful tool and virtually unavoidable in the world of modern publishing – who, for instance, wouldn't use Word's automatic formatting for footnotes? As a writer who remembers how tricky it was to lay out footnotes effectively on the page before there was such a tool, I couldn't imagine not using it. However, that otherwise wonderful footnoting function can introduce glitches, and footnotes have a nasty habit of suddenly disappearing (at the bottom of the page, not in the main text) as a complex document is edited and the program faces the challenge of rearranging notes and text on a rapidly changing page. The notes aren't usually actually gone and generally a little fiddling can bring them back, but there are instances where I've had to retype footnotes. Automatic referencing, on the other hand, can complicate the editing process, with in-text citations sometimes proving difficult to change, the reference list occasionally shifting position in a paper when the document is copied (into a clean copy after proofreading, for example) and the block format of the list preventing marginal comments on individual features of the references, which means that an editor or proofreader can only highlight and comment on the list as a whole, not on individual details within the list. This can result in a less precise and effective means of communication with both editors and proofreaders, so do keep that in mind when adding your citations and reference list.

There are many reasons, then, to maintain as much control over all aspects of your paper as possible. So when you use automatic formatting of any kind, use it sparingly and carefully, and treat it as a helpful tool, not as a substitute for your own discernment and sense of design.

PRS Tip:

There are simple ways to avoid or effectively use automatic formatting in Word without altering program settings. The following two will help you resolve problems I've mentioned above:

- *When you want to avoid the automatic numbering function in lists and headings, begin by typing a space on the line followed by the heading or item, then return to the beginning of the line and add the number before the space. Since it's when you add a space or return after a number that the automatic numbering kicks in, it won't apply if you enter the information in this way.*
- *If a footnote has disappeared from the bottom of the page, add a new footnote to the main text a few words before the number of the lost footnote. This usually nudges the program into remembering the lost footnote, which will reappear. Then you can delete the unnecessary note you added (or simply use the 'undo' button) and the lost note will remain, but in some documents this procedure may need to be repeated whenever the file is opened or major changes are made.*

Part III:
Communicating with Journal Editors: Submission, Acceptance, Revision and Rejection

CHAPTER 6
First Things First: Earning the Interest and Respect of an Academic or Scientific Editor

Impressing an academic or scientific editor in all the right ways is not an easy task. Even after you've considered all the aspects discussed above of designing, writing and presenting a top-notch scholarly paper for an appropriate and respected academic or scientific journal, you will need to invest a fair amount of time and effort into writing an eloquent covering letter that highlights both the unique achievements of your work and its relevance and topicality for the journal, preparing the initial elements of your article – title, abstract and keywords – with special (some might say obsessive) care and submitting your paper exactly as the journal indicates. Remember that you need to capture the attention of someone who is inundated with papers, abstracts and letters each and every day and whose job depends on making decisions that lead to the successful publication of quality scholarship. Think of that editor as a person desperately seeking a reason to reject rather than accept the work that crosses his or her desk, and the first impressions your writing makes as your initial line of defence: you need to convince that overworked editor that it would be a mistake not to consider your paper seriously, and ideally persuade him or her that your work will not only fit the journal's publishing agenda but stand out as exceptional among the many papers it publishes each year.

PART III: COMMUNICATING WITH JOURNAL EDITORS: SUBMISSION, ACCEPTANCE, REVISION AND REJECTION

6.1 Covering Letters: First Impressions

Although not all academic and scientific journals require a covering letter these days, many do and others will allow you to send one either as a separate document or as the first page of your paper. If the journal's guidelines offer you even the smallest opportunity to include a covering letter with your submission (or even if they don't suggest that you can't), send one, and while it's not a good idea to irritate an editor with a covering letter that's not wanted, even a brief (and beautifully written) paragraph or two in an email message will serve. A covering letter allows you to address the journal's editor directly and explain exactly what your work is, any aspects of it that are unique and important and the ways in which it is relevant to the journal's publishing agenda. As well as being informative, a covering letter is a sample of your writing, your persuasive skills and your professional perspective. It can make or break an article submission by either encouraging the editor to take a serious look at the paper itself or convincing him or her that there's no point in reading further.

It goes without saying that the language in which a covering letter is written should be correct in every way and a pleasure to read. A covering letter is not the place for grammatical or orthographic errors, awkward constructions, sloppy sentence structure or vague vocabulary. Avoid abbreviations and detailed data, and be sure to use terminology that is appropriate to the journal's focuses, keeping in mind both its range and specialisation. You want to let your reader know that you are an expert in your field and familiar with the terms and methods used in the research areas covered by the journal, but you don't want to lose that reader: remember that the editor making the initial decision as to whether your paper is worth serious consideration or not will know a great deal about the topics covered by the journal and have a very good idea of the kind of papers the journal is looking for, but may not be a specialist in your area. There was a time when most submission editors were experts in the topics of the papers they considered for publication, and with some publishers this is still the case, but it's rarer nowadays and often your paper won't pass under the eyes of specialists unless it makes it over the first hurdle and is sent on for peer review.

It can helpful both for you and for the editor if you suggest in your letter (or in your paper itself if the journal guidelines indicate it) a few researchers who would serve as appropriate reviewers of your work. Such suggestions will be taken with a grain of salt, of course, because an author can influence the results of reviews significantly by guiding an editor to use reviewers who are friends or colleagues, or certain to support his or her results or perspective. So it would be extraordinary for an editor to follow up on all your suggestions, but often one or more of the scholars you suggest will be contacted to review your paper, and simply by offering important names in your field and implying that you believe respected academics or scientists will assess your work positively you establish a professional and confident tone in your letter. Such a tone is essential to the success of a covering letter: your confidence in your research methods, results and argument needs to shine through your prose without (and this can be tricky) coming across as arrogance or misjudgement about the value of your work.

A precise and informative but brief explanation of exactly what your research is and why it is so important to both you and other scholars in your field will justify your confidence. You might want to indicate briefly, for instance, where your research fits into scholarship as a whole on the topic, how your methodology is reliable and/or innovative in relation to the approaches usually used in the area, the way in which your perspective differs from that of other researchers working in the field and/or how your theories and results are groundbreaking or at least important to scholarly and other communities. You only have so much room, however, and this material will need to be concise as well as eloquent, so it's important to be selective and lay particular emphasis on aspects of your work that will be of special interest to the journal, and thus to its editor.

It's also vital to get second opinions on your covering letter: when you're trying to make a large impression with a small number of words, it's easy even as a native speaker of a language to leave out essential details or generalise in inappropriate ways, so read and reread your letter yourself and then pass it along to colleagues, supervisors, fellow students, critical friends – anyone with knowledge in the area of your research or publication more generally who's willing to share an opinion on style and content. Prioritise responses when editing and polishing, but consider them all seriously – after all, you can anticipate which responses might be shared by the editor you're hoping to impress, but you simply can't predict an editor's thoughts with certainty, and any early hint of potential problems or misconceptions can be enormously helpful.

> *PRS Tip:*
> *Remember that the PRS team will always be delighted to proofread covering letters, book synopses (as well as the book itself), grant and thesis proposals, letters of recommendation, CVs and resumés, calls for papers, conference announcements and schedules, project summaries, publication lists, author biographies and any other kind of document, long or short, associated with academic or scientific research and publication.*

6.2   Titles, Abstracts and Keywords: Sound Connections

With the exception of your covering letter, the title, abstract and keywords of your paper are the first things encountered by the editor considering your submission (and the very first things if you're not able to submit any sort of covering letter). So although all parts of your paper demand your careful attention if your submission is to be successful, extra time and care invested in these three elements of your paper can reap a bountiful harvest. Think of your paper as dinner and its title, abstract and keywords as appetisers. You want the editor and the reviewers who will hopefully follow to be tantalised by your appetisers – to enjoy the texture and flavour of these delicacies while building a hearty appetite, and on that basis to expect good things from the dinner (paper) to follow. You do not want them to feel glutted by too much nourishment too richly seasoned or repulsed by a dull product of so low a quality that they leave the table before dinner arrives. This is to say that your title, abstract and keywords should hook the editor and inspire him or her to read on to the rest of your article.

6.2.1   The Very Beginning: The Title

Very few elements of an academic or scientific paper have to accomplish as much in as few words as the title does. The title is the first part of your paper read by the specialists who will review your article if it passes muster with the editor, and by the readers (usually more specialists in your field) who encounter it in the journal if you're fortunate enough to succeed in getting the paper published. According to the *APA Manual*, 'a title should summarize the main idea of the manuscript simply and, if possible, with style.'[5] For one, then, it should concisely inform your readers about the research you did in the study, mentioning the variables or theoretical issues you investigated in your paper and the relationship between them (e.g., 'Effect of Changing Weather Patterns on Home Insurance Policies'), and it can also hint at what you discovered (e.g., 'Effect of Changing Weather Patterns on Home Insurance Policies: Clients Left Out in the Cold?'). Secondly, it should do both in an interesting and engaging way that allows the language you use to carry nuances and allusions (perhaps even a little word play) while providing the necessary details with precision: the word 'Cold' in the second example above, for instance, not only refers to the unpleasant physical reality of those who lose their homes due to natural disasters but also implies a certain lack of warmth on the part of insurance companies who do not provide support in such situations. The subtitle as a whole hints at the nature of the results, with the question mark leaving the matter uncertain and the reader whose sympathy or curiosity has been tweaked eager (one hopes) to discover the answer and thus well primed to read on.

---

[5] *The Publication Manual of the American Psychological Association*, 6th ed. (Washington, DC: American Psychological Association, 2010), 23.

However, titles are also best if they're as short as possible, and many style manuals and journal guidelines set strict word or character limits on titles. The *APA Manual*, for instance, recommends limiting the title of an academic or scientific article to 12 words or less, which renders the second (and to my mind more engaging) of my two examples above too long at 15 words. There are, then, both practical and creative reasons for avoiding all unnecessary words in your title: adverbs and adjectives are rarely necessary and should be used sparingly and to maximum effect ('Changing' in my title above, for instance, alludes to changes in both the weather and the coverage provided by insurance policies), while words such as 'study,' 'method' and 'results' are almost always extraneous in that they serve no useful purpose and can simply burden a title and render it more awkward: 'Results Suggest that Clients Might Be Left Out in the Cold' says basically the same thing as the subtitle I have above, but it uses almost twice as many words and simply isn't as catchy. Do check the journal guidelines on this, however, as some journals aren't averse to longer titles and a few even ask that the type of study or methodology be identified in the title as a subtitle (or even a secondary subtitle, though to be honest, using two colons in a title isn't an English style I'd recommend) along the lines of 'A Study Protocol' or 'A Randomised Trial.'

It may be tempting to use abbreviations in your title – an acronym is counted as one word, after all, no matter how many words it abbreviates – but it's better to avoid them, and many style manuals and journal guidelines will ask that you do. With some terms, however, the abbreviations are better known than the full version (IQ, for instance, and AIDS), so in such cases they are probably appropriate for the title: few publishers would expect you to use 'intelligence quotient' instead of IQ in your title. If you find that you absolutely have to use abbreviations in your title, be sure that they are relatively common and will be familiar to the journal's audience: indeed, all terminology you use in your title should be appropriate to the audience you anticipate, because I can assure you that feeling lost before you've even made it through the title is a frustrating reading experience. Be sure to observe any patterns of capitalisation required by the journal to which you're submitting your paper, and the same is the case with font style and size, the use of punctuation (a colon or a dash between title and subtitle, for example), the placement of the title in relation to other parts of the paper (on a separate page, at the top of the paper or both), and the format of any running heading that may be required. Your title contains only a few of the many words in your paper, but it's right up at the top for the world (including editors) to see, so you want to make it perfect in terms of language and format, and keep it short and interesting as well.

6.2.2 Summing It All Up: The Abstract

While covering letters are required less often with today's online submission procedures than they once were, the need for an abstract when submitting an academic or scientific article is more common, even in disciplines that once would not have used such an initial summary of the paper to follow. So in most cases it's best to plan on including an abstract from the beginning, regardless of your subject and field, and to recognise that a good abstract, like a good covering letter or a good introduction, requires a lot of consideration and you will likely need to return to it and make adjustments a few times before it's finished. It's useful to draft your abstract early in the writing process, as it can help you focus on the essential elements of your research and results as you work on your paper, but your abstract will certainly need to be edited and rewritten once your paper is finished, and probably again after you've had a colleague or other qualified reader look it over for you, which is highly recommended in the case of an abstract. As with your title, it's virtually impossible to put too much time and effort into improving and polishing your abstract because it is often amidst the abstract that an editor is either won or lost, and the situation is similar after publication, when readers often decide whether to read your entire paper or not on the basis of the abstract they find through an online (or other kind of) search. So the abstract of a paper can be the most important part of an article, for good or ill.

An academic or scientific abstract should summarise the contents of the paper it precedes briefly and comprehensively. It should not contain information that isn't present in the paper and it should report, not evaluate, what can be found in the paper. Like the title, the abstract needs to be precise, concise and as engaging as possible, but it also needs to be densely packed with information. Word limits for abstracts set by journals usually range between 100 and 300 words, with 150-250 the most common length, and those limits should be strictly observed despite how much must be accomplished in that short space. A carefully prepared abstract will situate your research in both its physical and intellectual contexts; it will inform the reader about the problem(s) or concept(s) you're investigating, any participants in your study and the essential features of the methodology used; and it will report the basic findings, implications and conclusions of your study. Each abstract will therefore also be unique, so exactly what should or should not be included in an abstract varies from author to author and paper to paper.

Some style manuals and journal guidelines will provide detailed instructions on the kind of information that should be included in your abstract. The *APA Manual*, for example, gives sound practical advice as well as outlining the expectations of abstracts for a variety of different kinds of paper such as empirical studies, literature reviews, theory-oriented papers and case studies. An APA abstract is a single paragraph, but in many journal guidelines detailed advice on the content of abstracts will come in the form of instructions for a structured abstract – that is, an abstract divided into short sections or paragraphs, usually with individual headings such as Background, Methods, Participants, Results, Conclusion and the like, often in bold or italic font. The headings can differ from journal to journal and also according to the type of paper, so be sure to check the guidelines carefully and to identify correctly what type of paper you've written before finalising the structure and layout of your abstract. Some journals will even specify the length of each section of the abstract, but in most cases the balance of information will be yours to determine, and even in a completely structured abstract you will need to decide which concepts, methods and results to include. This decision should be based not just on what you think most important about your research and the article it's generated but also what you think the journal editor will find most appropriate and engaging for his or her readers.

It is crucial, of course, that your abstract is well written in grammatically correct, properly punctuated and complete English sentences. Every sentence should bear the maximum amount of information and meaning possible, with minimal use of minor words, and each main word should be chosen with great care, primarily for its denotations, of course, but also for its potential connotations: it should be precise and informative, and if it manages to nuance matters in a way that seems appropriate to your results and the journal's interests, that's a good thing, too. Your first sentence in particular is crucial to gaining the interest and confidence of your reader: it needs to be polished to perfection in both content and style so that it reads smoothly and clearly communicates important points about your work. As a general rule, avoid references in an abstract unless essential; use abbreviations only if they're absolutely necessary (and not at all if the guidelines prevent it) and clearly define each one (other than those for common measures) that you do have to use; and beware of too much specialised terminology and jargon – some will perhaps be necessary to explain your methods and results, but while you want your readers to know that you're aware of the correct terms and how to use them, you don't want to confuse or lose readers who are, necessarily, not yet familiar with the content of your paper. What you do want is for them, and especially that all-important editor, to read on, so everything about your abstract should encourage that possibility.

PRS Tip:
Abstracts can often require a lot of attention during and after proofreading, especially if you're not a native speaker of English and find yourself struggling to condense the contents of your paper into carefully structured sentences that express your ideas with precision. If you have to rewrite your abstract to a significant degree after having your paper read by a PRS proofreader (or any other careful, critical reader), you may want to send it back for a second read. You can always send just the abstract and/or any other particularly problematic part of your paper, and request the same proofreader to double-check your revisions or a different one if you'd like a second opinion. It's a good way to reduce the cost of final proofreading while buying peace of mind before submitting your work.

6.2.3 Searching for the Right Terms: The Keywords

For such a small part of your paper, the keywords pack a very large punch and in today's world of digital publication in which journal articles are available worldwide via the internet, some might argue that a paper's keywords are even more important than a paper's title. In one sense, perhaps they are: certainly, it is easier to include in the keywords the terms you think readers are likely to use when searching for information on the topics covered in your paper because that's precisely why the keywords are included and there's no need to join them syntactically into the logical sense one expects of a title. However, your title is also a tool for facilitating your readers' successful discovery of your article once it's published and available online, and so is your abstract: by embedding keywords in your title and abstract you increase your readers' ability to find them via those keywords, and in your abstract in particular you have a lot of room to include essential terms through which your potential readers might search for information of the very kind that your paper presents. So choose the words you use in your abstract and title with the same care and eye to searchability as you do the keywords themselves.

The number of keywords recommended or allowed is almost always indicated in journal guidelines, with three usually being the minimum and five to eight the maximum. Some journals will want you to list your keywords alphabetically, separate them with commas or semi-colons, use an initial capital on each term or not, and otherwise format them in particular ways, so consult the instructions before finalising your list. Acronyms are usually acceptable as keywords, especially if the acronym is well known or is likely to be used as a search word by the readers you're targeting, but connective words (e.g., 'and,' 'or,' 'between,' etc.) are often frowned upon because they serve little purpose and can vary considerably in the phrases used as search tools, which means that they can potentially hinder instead of helping potential readers when they are searching for papers just like yours. By choosing appropriate keywords and using them effectively in other parts of your paper, you increase the possibility of your paper being more widely read and cited and thus increase your chances of achieving the effect you would wish for your article. At the same time, you help increase the readers and ratings of the journal that has published your paper, which makes for a win-win situation (see also Section 2.1.2 above).

6.3 Ready and Willing: Submission Procedures

Ideally, you will have familiarised yourself with the journal's submission procedures before or while preparing your paper, so will already have formatted the different parts of your paper in appropriate ways and used the right type of files, but when you find yourself ready to submit, you should check all submission requirements again to be sure you've not missed any details and double-check your paper and other files to be sure they conform to the requirements in every way. Ignoring the specifics of a journal's instructions about how articles should be submitted is an effective technique for irritating an editor before he or she has read even a single word of your work, so you need to do your best to ensure that you don't give that editor any reason to believe that aspects of your paper might not conform to journal requirements and thus decide not to read it (or even your covering letter) at all. In many cases, not meeting the submission requirements will simply win you a request to resubmit appropriately, but that takes time and patience on both your part and that of the journal's staff, as well as potential revisions, so it's best to get it right the first time and immediately establish a professional and productive relationship with the journal in which you're hoping to be published.

Although there are journals which accept multiple submissions – that is, that are willing to consider papers that are simultaneously submitted to other journals as well – this is rare among academic and scientific journals, often considered somewhat unethical and best avoided. Conscientious editors and reviewers spend a great deal of time on your paper, generally on the assumption that you genuinely want to publish your work in their journal and that their views are important to you. If you submit your paper to several journals with the intention of publishing it in the one that gives you the best review, you not only diminish the value of the effort invested by the editors and reviewers who read your article, but may also tend to ignore what might be valid and valuable criticisms of your paper – criticisms that if taken seriously and accommodated in revisions would improve your paper. A better and more professional practice (if somewhat more time-consuming) is to submit to one journal and only submit to a second one if the response from the first is a simple rejection or requires revisions that you feel after careful reflection would be inappropriate for your work. If you do feel the need to submit your paper to more than one journal at once, be sure to inform each journal of this fact in your covering letter. It's also good in this case to set a deadline in your letter – three months after submission, for instance – by which you'll be hoping to hear back before making a final decision about which journal to choose, but be aware that in some cases this can backfire and make your paper a lower priority than a paper that has been sent exclusively to one journal.

Most academic and scientific journals now accept and many of them insist on online submission. If you're new to this process and find aspects of it confusing, send your questions along to the email address that is usually provided as a contact for submission queries. It's far better to ask and have your questions clarified than to complete the process incorrectly or give up and attempt to submit in ways no longer acceptable to many journals (in a print copy via postal mail, for instance). Be sure that your documents are in the correct file formats – Word is among the preferences of most journals, but there will often be other options as well. Sometimes figures (and occasionally large tables) will need to be sent as separate files either in the same file format as the main document or prepared via a different program, so be sure to prepare and submit them just as the guidelines indicate, taking into consideration whether they will be reproduced in black and white or colour in print, online or both. Take care, too, with the placement of tables and figures within your main paper if the guidelines suggest that this is acceptable because journals differ considerably in terms of where they want tables and figures positioned within a manuscript (see Section 5.1 above).

Special attention should also be paid to any submission requirements associated with blind peer reviewing. If the journal uses blind peer reviews to assess papers prior to publication, its guidelines will usually contain some specific instructions as to what authors are expected to do in order to ensure that their identities will not be known to the specialists reviewing their writing. Requirements differ, but can include ensuring that the name of the author (or names of the authors if there are more than one) and any other personal information do not appear on the title page included with the paper, which usually means that a title page (or other short document) with that personal information will need to be submitted separately; that any sources written by the author of the submitted paper that are cited in the paper and listed among the references should be referred to in such a way that a reader cannot determine that the same author is responsible for the paper currently under consideration (any passages that you need to alter to meet this requirement can be changed back once the paper is accepted for publication); and that any author identification should be removed from the properties of the files you submit. If you do not observe such requirements, your paper will be returned, at least for revisions, before it can be reviewed, so care with such details the first time around will better facilitate a successful review process.

Do not exceed any word limits indicated for the article as a whole or for any particular section of the paper, such as the abstract, and be aware that word limits may differ according to type of paper in some journal guidelines, so read them carefully. While many editors will not be put off by a good paper that slightly exceeds word counts and such a minor discrepancy can be sorted out during final editing, a journal that wants papers of about 25 pages or perhaps 10,000 words does not want papers of 50 pages or 20,000 words. Do include a covering letter if this is permitted (see Section 6.1 above) and any other supporting documents that may be required, such as an author biography, a list of previous publications or a CV. You may need to number any files you're submitting (and the pages within them) in whatever ways the guidelines indicate, and label or name them according to the instructions as well (including running headings within the documents). Finally, remember to send along with your submission any processing or reviewing fees that may be required at this point: your paper will not be considered without them. As a general rule, the more you can do to meet the journal's requirements in each and every way, the better chance you have that your paper will be greeted with a positive attitude.

PRS Tip:
It's always good to leave yourself a little extra time between finishing your paper and actually submitting it. A day or two or, better still, a week can provide enough distance to allow you a more objective perspective on work in which you've necessarily been immersed for some time. So if you can, set your paper and all accompanying documents aside for a bit and return to read them on a day when you have enough time to read through everything carefully at one sitting. Often errors, awkward phrases and inconsistent terminology and formatting unnoticed for days or even weeks will suddenly leap off the page when you give yourself this sort of opportunity to be a thoughtful, critical reader of your own writing.

CHAPTER 7
After Submission: Acceptance, Rejection and Revision

Waiting for a response from a journal to which you've submitted the paper that has cost you so much hard work and careful attention can feel like a time of limbo, so patience is required. You can use this time, however, to reflect on and record any alterations that come to mind as you agonise over whether you really did get everything right or not. Avoid changing any of the documents or files you actually sent to the journal, because they represent the versions of your work that you and the journal will be working with in the future if the response you receive is positive. Recording any ideas for changes in a separate note file associated with your original files can, however, be a useful way of keeping yourself in touch with your paper and preparing yourself for any revisions that may be necessary.

7.1   'Just What We're Looking For':
The Successful Publishing Relationship

This is, of course, the response that every scholar would like to receive each time he or she submits a paper for publication. Unfortunately, that's not the case, but for those fortunate enough to find a suitable home for their work at once, celebration is in order, so do take the opportunity to give yourself a well-deserved pat on the back – it's not a small accomplishment to publish your work successfully in a reputable journal in today's highly competitive publishing environment. Do not, however, consider your work done. Even when a journal immediately accepts a paper for publication, the acceptance is often accompanied by requests for revisions. These tend to be minor, but that doesn't mean they're unimportant to the journal's editor, and there will also be proofs to tend to and perhaps other requirements depending on the journal.

Remember that despite your elation (and perhaps an overwhelming urge to hug the editor who sends you the good news) you should remain completely professional in your correspondence. Reply immediately, express your gratitude and excitement (within reason) about being published in the journal and your willingness to comply with any requirements that have been mentioned, whether general to all authors or specific to your paper. Only if you find that a request to make changes in your paper is impossible to accommodate should you refuse to make them, and then it's best not to do so outright, but to explain carefully and courteously which requests present a problem and exactly why. If it's unclear to you why such requests have been made, politely ask if the editor could explain the reason behind the requests more thoroughly. Similarly, if you've decided since you first submitted your paper that changes are needed, explain them carefully in your reply, describing in detail why you believe the changes necessary and what you intend to do to fix the problems: developments in relevant scholarship or updates of publishing information for sources are, for instance, valid and common reasons for changes. Be flexible and willing to compromise whenever possible with regard to revisions whether they are initiated by you or your editor, and do not wait to share your intentions or your changes until the copyediting or proof stage. Generally, at the proof stage revisions are very expensive and the only changes that can be made are corrections of errors; some publishers will charge authors for changes made this late in the game, even those that both author and editor deem absolutely necessary, and such changes can quickly become very expensive.

All requests from the journal whether major or minor should be dealt with in a timely fashion and all deadlines (for reading and correcting proofs, for instance) should be met. Journals usually work on very tight schedules, and you want your work published sooner rather than later. Keep the doors of communication open as you're working toward final publication, and be sure to explain (and justify) any problems you're facing that may make it difficult for you to comply with any requirements or to do so in the time frame set by the journal. Any fees for publication of your paper or for printing figures in colour (which tends to be expensive and cost extra) should be paid as soon as they are due. However, as such fees can often be paid by your university, subsidised through membership or taken from research grants or scholarship funds, do explore those avenues before sending along your credit card number: publication fees for some journals can be very high these days, and institutional support of scholarly publication is usually expected by journals as much as it is desired by academic and scientific authors.

7.2   When 'No' Means No:
Professional Departures and New Beginnings

As an undergraduate, I and some fellow students once attended a dinner party at which one of our most respected professors confessed that she had earned a D grade in a university-level philosophy course. I suspect that we would never have heard such shocking news had tongues not been well loosened by the wine that was flowing in celebration of exams coming to an end, and only later did I realise how interesting and encouraging a confession it was as we all anxiously awaited our grades. The person who made it was, after all, a tenured full professor, she had designed and directed a women's studies programme for years and was both well respected and well published in her field. She concluded her confession with words that are well worth considering when faced with a rejection letter from a journal or any other publisher: "So you see, there is academic life after a D!" My fellow students and I shared some meaningful looks and a moment of sombre reflection, but all of us (the professor with the near-failing grade included) were very soon laughing and moving on to other things.

I'm not suggesting that laughter is an appropriate response to a rejection letter (or often an email message these days, but I'll stick to 'letter' here), or that you will feel remotely like laughing when faced with such bad news (unless, of course, you decide to imbibe a good deal of wine yourself, which may or may not be advisable). I am suggesting, however, that there is a successful publication career after having your writing rejected by an editor. J. K. Rowling apparently received over 50 rejections before a publisher finally accepted the first in her series of best-selling Harry Potter books – I often wonder how many of those publishers have since used those volumes to knock themselves over the head – and virtually every successful publishing academic or scientist has experienced at least one letter of rejection over the years. Unfortunately, letters of rejection can be terribly impersonal, and while this is a helpful reminder that writing and publishing are business and rejections are not personal, it can also be maddening. Receiving a rejection letter, for instance, that curtly states that your paper does not fit the journal's publishing agenda when you know very well from your research on the journal that it does indeed fit that agenda provides no real reason for the rejection and no advice for improvement. Such a rejection can be frustrating and unhelpful, but it's simply a quick, general way of saying 'no thank you' and a very good indication that it's time to move on to a different journal. Although there are always exceptions, there is little point in demanding explanations in such an incommunicative environment, and a good chance of shining a poor light on a relationship with a journal that could in the future still be a likely candidate for submissions.

If the letter provides something a little more helpful by suggesting, for instance, that your work is interesting, but your article would be more appropriate for a more specialised journal or perhaps just the opposite, that your paper would be a better fit for a less specialised journal, that, too, is usually an example of 'no' meaning no. In such cases, it's best simply to move on and resubmit elsewhere, taking into consideration while choosing a new journal (see Section 2.1 above) any specific comments the editor might have offered. Whenever in doubt about whether a response is a rejection or a conditional acceptance (which I discuss below), have a colleague who's worked with editors and publishers take a look at the letter. A less than positive reply from an editor is not the type of news one wants to share, of course, but a second opinion from a knowledgeable, trustworthy friend can be extremely helpful at this point.

7.3   'We're Interested but…': The Revision Process

Many rejection letters can be read in a more positive light as constructive criticism that can help improve papers and the scholarship in them, and even as conditional acceptance letters, though some would argue that there is a clear distinction between rejection and conditional acceptance that resides in that all-important 'but' in the heading above. A letter that explicitly states that it will accept a paper if (and only if) the conditions it lays out – these are generally problems to be resolved – are met, sometimes within a set amount of time, is a conditional acceptance. A letter that lays out a number of problems to be resolved in your paper if the editor is to consider or reconsider it isn't quite a conditional acceptance, but very nearly so. A letter that rejects your paper and provides very specific reasons for so doing isn't a conditional acceptance either, but it holds out some hope.

Determining whether you should or should not revise your paper to resolve the problems indicated in a response from a journal editor can be difficult, even if the letter says that your paper will be published if you make the changes. If an editor's demands mean that an author would need to compromise what he or she believes to be the integrity of his or her research, data and/or argument, for example, a scholar is well advised to consider the matter carefully. If acceptance after complying is not a certainty, it may be best to move along to another journal first, and if acceptance is a certainty after conditions are met it may prove necessary to write a carefully crafted response explaining what can and cannot be changed and why. If a compromise can be negotiated with the editor, even ethical and intellectual hurdles can be surmounted.

Just as each paper is unique, each letter from an editor is unique, and reading information that you really would rather not have received at all with an open, objective and thoughtful mind, especially when your own writing is the focus, can be difficult. After first reading a disappointing letter from an editor, regardless of whether it is a rejection or a call for revision, it's best to set it aside (or close the email message) and take some time to calm down and regain distance. Go for a walk or enjoy a bubble bath, eat some ice cream or work out at the gym, watch a funny movie or read some Jane Austen – whatever it takes to soften the blow and bring you to a more objective perspective. Then read the letter again with your focus on understanding exactly what about your paper was criticised and what sort of suggestions might have been offered for improvements. Have an experienced colleague – ideally one who read or is willing to read your paper for you – read the letter as well and offer ideas. Then reread your paper critically paying special attention to any details or sections singled out as problematic in the letter. Some decisions about how to proceed with revisions will be much more complicated than others, and each situation unique, but below you'll find a brief discussion of three main categories of criticism that often arise in the letters academic and scientific authors receive from editors.

7.3.1   Formatting, Structure and Referencing Style

One of the easiest forms of criticism to deal with is that addressing noncompliance with journal guidelines regarding the formatting, structure and referencing style used in a paper. If, for instance, the letter you've received informs you that you haven't followed the journal guidelines in the structure and layout of your paper, in the formatting of your tables or perhaps in the citation and referencing style you've used, and those are the only problems mentioned, they can be easily resolved. If the letter is a conditional acceptance based on your improving these aspects of your paper, then it's simply a matter of complying (see Chapters 3 & 5 of this *Guide*). Reply to the editor with thanks for the helpful criticism and explain that you understand the problems, are beginning revisions and will be sending the edited paper back as soon as possible (or within a certain time frame if one has been given).

Because it takes a good deal of work to reformat a paper carefully, however, and the format required differs considerably from journal to journal, it's a good idea to be certain that reformatting for the same journal will be worth the effort. So if the letter you received only suggests that the editor might reconsider your paper if you resolve the problems identified, or simply points out the problems as the reason for not accepting the paper, it would be best if you wish to continue pursuing publication with the journal to confirm that your efforts will in fact result in serious consideration. Reply to the editor with thanks for the helpful criticism, explain that you understand the problems, and ask if he or she would be willing to reconsider or accept the paper were you to correct those problems (see Letter A.1 in the Appendix below). If the answer you get back is promising, it's probably well worth revising your paper and resubmitting to the same journal. You've opened the door to a positive working relationship and shown your willingness to work toward publication, but you're going to need to do the job of complying with the journal guidelines much more carefully and accurately this time. You've been given a second chance, and it would be unwise to make the same mistake twice – that an editor will remember.

Whether you're resubmitting your paper on the basis of a conditional acceptance or a conditional reconsideration, explain in detail in a letter accompanying your resubmission exactly what you've done to improve your formatting, structure and/or referencing style, and address each and every concern itemised in the letter you received (see Letter A.2 in the Appendix below). If there was anything that proved problematic or any ways in which you weren't able to comply with the guidelines or specific requests, mention them and why the problems couldn't be resolved as you'd hoped. It's always good to suggest as well your willingness to revise further if need be.

7.3.2   Language and Clarity

Somewhat more challenging to deal with is criticism regarding the accuracy, clarity and style of your written English, especially as this problem can often result in misunderstanding or misinterpretation of your work, which can also lead to criticism of the sort discussed in Section 7.3.3. Any author who takes his or her work seriously enough to prepare and polish it for publication is working to communicate effectively, so if that communication has failed in some way, it can be difficult to determine how to proceed. For the most part, if it is the clarity and style of your writing that's the problem, especially if it's been pointed out by more than one editor, you simply need to revise to improve your English writing. The approaches to replying to the editor I've outlined above regarding formatting, structural and referencing issues (Section 7.3.1) apply here as well (with a focus on language, of course), but whether you manage to earn a conditional acceptance or a conditional reconsideration or neither, you are almost certainly going to need to revise your paper before submitting it again to the same or any other journal.

As you're working to improve your English and your article, you may find Chapter 4 of this *Guide* particularly helpful, and perhaps Section 3.2 as well. If you were fortunate enough to receive some detailed commentary from the editor about the writing problems in your paper, review those constructions or words or areas carefully and read through your paper as a whole with your eye alert to occurrences of any incorrect patterns mentioned by the editor. If the letter you received doesn't provide such helpful advice, you will need to review your prose more carefully still, and in this case it is probably best to seek a second and perhaps a third opinion. A specialist in your field who has published in English is a good choice, and so is a native speaker of English – a colleague or fellow student if possible, or a professional academic or scientific proofreader. As with revisions to formatting, structure and references, when you resubmit to the same journal be sure to explain precisely what you've done to improve your writing, including any use of professional proofreaders, as this can show the editor the effort you've made to improve your paper and speak volumes about your willingness to do what has to be done to achieve successful publication.

PRS Tip:

If you're dealing with requested revisions to the formatting, structure, references and/or language of your paper, the proofreading team at PRS can help a great deal. Once you have your paper revised and your explanation of what you've done to meet the journal's requirements composed, send us both documents along with links to the guidelines and we'll proofread them carefully to ensure that your revisions clarify your writing and meet the requirements, and that your explanation of them accurately describes the changes you've made. You can use the track changes function in Word as you revise if you'd like to show your proofreader exactly what you've done, and if you've been unable to resolve any problems, you can highlight them in your paper with marginal comments so your proofreader will know to pay special attention to those areas or concerns. Sometimes clients even send along the version of the paper bearing the editor's or reviewer's comments, and that can be helpful for clarifying problems as well. After we've proofread your paper and accompanying documents, remember to request a certificate stating that your document has been proofread by PRS. This will further demonstrate to the editor the efforts you've made to improve your paper and meet the journal's requirements.

7.3.3 Content: Methods, Data and Argument

This can be the most difficult of all kinds of criticism to deal with because it cuts at the heart of a paper. Language problems can contribute to problems with your methods, data and argument, and so can formatting, structural and referencing issues – it's all one intricate weave, after all, just like that tightrope. In some instances, however, an editor (or reviewers) will detect more fundamental problems with the methodology of a study, the theories adopted, the data or analysis presented and/or the argument constructed by an author. It can take a careful and open-minded review of your own paper and research in relation to the critical comments you've received

– a thorough critical self-assessment, as it were – to decide exactly how to interpret such criticism. Are the problems raised evidence that the editor's perspective is simply far removed from your own and the journal just not the right fit? Or are they valid concerns about real shortcomings or flaws in your research that taken constructively could facilitate the improvement of your article in fundamental ways? If the first is the case, it would probably be best to submit your paper to a different journal: if you believe your research to be valid and valuable, it's your responsibility to publish it despite disagreement. If the second is the case, then your paper almost certainly needs revision and it might be unethical to submit it to another journal without resolving the problems identified in the letter you've received.

Each case is unique, of course, and you will have to decide for yourself how best to proceed, ideally with some advice from one or more specialists in your field. Academic advisors and supervisors can be particularly helpful, and so can fellow students and colleagues, but ultimately the sorts of changes needed to resolve problems with methods, data and argument tend to be ones that only the author can choose and make. Sometimes it's a matter of explaining more carefully key issues such as the relationships and controls considered in your study, or presenting more clearly the evidence gleaned from your research, or stating more explicitly the limitations and shortcomings of your approaches and data. In other instances you may need to clarify what is innovative and significant about your research to justify your methods and results: often ideas and approaches that move beyond conventional wisdom need to be stated more clearly and more often than one might expect. These matters overlap with language problems, and reflecting critically before you revise on both what you need to tell your readers and the language in which you share that information will often improve your paper immensely.

More fundamental are criticisms suggesting that the paper you've submitted is too preliminary or not a minimum publishable unit (see Section 1.4), which means that it's not a complete study – it doesn't quite tell the whole story needed for an original research paper, for instance – so you'll need to develop your argument further before resubmitting, and perhaps provide additional evidence, whether you choose to stick with the same journal or not. Similarly critical of the overall argument of your study is the comment that your paper is 'descriptive.' Research papers necessarily describe procedures and observations, but they need to do much more than that, so to call a paper 'descriptive' is to suggest that the author has not used the data presented in the paper to develop a coherent argument – it lacks, for example, a hypothesis or thesis and a clear line of logic by which that hypothesis or thesis is tested through research and/or trials. This is the sort of problem that requires a return to the drawing board to rethink your purpose in writing and redesign your argument. Sometimes starting your paper again (cutting and pasting in the useful bits of information from your first version as necessary) is the best route in such cases. If the criticism you've received suggests that your data is either insufficient or unconvincing, or your experiments or means of analysis are flawed, or necessary controls are inadequate or absent, you'll need to reflect on the nature of your methodology and results. Sometimes presenting the material differently can make a great difference, but this sort of criticism is an indication that you may need to repeat or restructure basic elements of your research.

In all decisions you make about revising the content of your paper you should carefully weigh your options with a focus on what is best for you and your work as well as for the journal in which you'd like to see your paper published. Seeking knowledgeable advice is vital and giving yourself enough time to digest the criticism offered by the editor and/or reviewers as well as to conduct a careful, objective review of your work is essential. If you decide to revise in order to resolve the problems identified in the letter you received and resubmit to the same journal, you can reply to the editor using the approaches I've outlined in the section on formatting, structure and referencing above (7.3.1). Explain in your initial reply that you've considered the criticism offered and describe how you're planning to revise the content of your paper to resolve the problems identified. This may well involve explaining what you can't change as well as what you can, so be sure to clarify and justify your reasoning regarding any noncompliance with the journal's requests, remembering that you need to convince the editor and/or reviewers why your view on these points is a valid one. If you earn a conditional acceptance or reconsideration, you want to be sure that it's been given on the basis of what you actually can do to meet the journal's needs while maintaining the integrity of your research. That way, when you resubmit your paper, the changes you've made and explained again in your new covering letter will be expected and an indication of your ability to work effectively with the journal to achieve publication, rather than an unwanted surprise.

Persistence can reap rewards and is a necessary skill for an academic or scientist (or any other author) who wishes to publish his or her writing, but just as there are times when a particular publishing venue such as an academic or scientific journal has to be passed over in placing your work appropriately, so there are papers that may need to be abandoned, or perhaps completely reconceived and rewritten. A paper in which the editor (and perhaps the reviewers) of a reputable top-tier journal has found significant flaws is a good candidate for such treatment. Even this, however, is a form of progress and can be seen in a positive light. That same creative writing teacher who insisted on the primary importance of perspective always urged his students to move on to the next project because, as he asserted, an author tends to keep writing the same story again and again in various forms, and only by moving on to the next manifestation will he or she ever get that story (close to) right.

On a loftier note, Augustine of Hippo, a master of eloquence and pillar of the Western philosophical tradition, confessed in a letter that he endeavoured to be "one of those authors who write as they make progress and make progress by their writing," and thus he welcomed criticism: "if I set down something with insufficient forethought or knowledge, it deserves to be condemned, not only by those who see it, but even by me."[6] Given that about 5,000,000 of Augustine's words still survive for us today and that his numerous texts have inspired lively debate and profoundly influenced authors, scholars and leaders for nearly 2,000 years, he may have a valid point. So the gold to be mined here is focus on your intellectual progress and keep writing!

[6] John Leinenweber, trans., *Letters of Saint Augustine* (Tarrytown, NY: Triumph Books, 1992), 148.

PRS Tip:

We'd love to keep proofreading what you're writing. If you (or your colleagues or students) are interested in our service and would like more information, please visit our web site at:
www.proof-reading-service.com

The PRS team is more than happy to answer questions and provide any help you may need 24 hours a day from Monday to Friday.

You can reach us by email at:
enquiries@proof-reading-service.com

or via the following phone numbers:
+44 (0) 20 31 500 431
+1 (202) 534-3925
+886 (0)919 354 605

When you send us your next document for proofreading, please use our drop box at:
https://www.hightail.com/u/CEDS.

This is a much safer way than email to submit work, although we will certainly accept documents by email if you prefer. Please remember that you can pay for our services (via Paypal or Sagepay) and print and download invoices and receipts through our payment portal. When you send us a document for proofreading, we'll send you the login details with your confirmation email.

We hope to hear from you soon!

Sample Responses to Letters from Academic and Scientific Editors

Each letter to an editor is unique, so the following letters are only examples, but they will provide you with ideas about how to format and word your own replies to academic and scientific editors. The letters are completely fictional, with invented names and situations. The complete addresses may not be necessary if you're communicating with an editor via email, as is so often the case these days, but I've included them to show the layout of a formal letter. For your own mailing address, it would be best to use university or department letterhead if available and provide your personal name, phone number and email address beneath the letterhead.

The first letter (A.1) posits that the editor is interested in the article and thinks it appropriate for the journal, but has pointed out a number of problems with the formatting, structure and referencing style of the paper as the reason for not accepting it. Whether or not the paper will be reconsidered or accepted if the necessary revisions are done remains uncertain, so the letter aims to confirm that the paper will be seriously reconsidered and ideally accepted if the necessary changes are made. It does this by thanking the editor for his helpful advice, indicating that the author understands the problems and is in the process of correcting them, and asking whether the editor would like to reconsider the paper for publication.

Assuming that the first letter received a positive response, the second letter (A.2) is designed to accompany the revised paper once all the necessary changes to formatting, structure and referencing have been made. It explains exactly what's been done to correct the problems, addressing all of the concerns about the format, structure and references raised by the editor. It also explains one change that may prove problematic and offers an alternative solution. Finally, it verifies that a professional proofreader has checked the article and indicates a willingness on the part of the author to make any further changes that may be necessary to facilitate successful publication.

Letter A.1: Earning or Confirming Serious Reconsideration or Conditional Acceptance

Dr Sandra Jones
Department of Social Sciences
University of the Pacific Coast
P.O. Box 101
Salmon Cove, British Columbia
V2K 3L4   Canada
(609) 741-8955
sandra.jones@univpaccoast.ca

Mr Reginald Smith, Editor
Journal of Changing Weather
P.O. Box 707
River Rapids, Oregon
76545   USA
(972) 861-9805
smith.editor@jchangweath.com

March 3, 2014

Dear Mr Smith,

Thank you for your letter regarding my manuscript entitled "Effect of Changing Weather Patterns on Home Insurance Policies: Clients Left Out in the Cold?" I'm delighted that you're interested in the paper and think it might be appropriate for the *Journal of Changing Weather*.

I very much appreciate the time and effort you've put into your comments. Your advice about the formatting, structure and referencing style of my paper is most helpful. I've looked over the *Journal of Changing Weather* author guidelines again and see exactly where I've gone wrong and what changes need to be made. Once I've made the necessary revisions, I plan to have the paper professionally proofread to ensure that I've met all the requirements consistently.

However, I remain unsure about whether you're willing to reconsider the article once the necessary changes have been made, so I'm hoping you can confirm that you'd like me to send you the revised paper for reconsideration or publication. I've begun working on the revisions already and will be able to return the article to you within a couple of weeks.

With thanks for your time and assistance,

[sign here for a formal letter]

Sandra Jones

Letter A.2: Resubmitting a Paper after Necessary Revisions Have Been Made

Dr Sandra Jones
Department of Social Sciences
University of the Pacific Coast
P.O. Box 101
Salmon Cove, British Columbia
V2K 3L4   Canada
(609) 741-8955
sandra.jones@univpaccoast.ca

Mr Reginald Smith, Editor
Journal of Changing Weather
P.O. Box 707
River Rapids, Oregon
76545   USA
(972) 861-9805
smith.editor@jchangweath.com

March 15, 2014

Dear Mr Smith,

Further to our correspondence a couple of weeks ago, I'm attaching the revised version of my article entitled "Effect of Changing Weather Patterns on Home Insurance Policies: Clients Left Out in the Cold?" I have now completed all of the changes you requested:

- The numerical style of in-text referencing has been changed to author-date referencing in APA style.

- The list of references has been arranged alphabetically by the last names of authors instead of numerically, and other changes to conform to APA style have been made to the references.
- The article has been restructured to include separate Limitations and Conclusions sections.
- All headings and subheadings have been adjusted to conform to the requirements indicated in the *Journal of Changing Weather* author guidelines, including the removal of numbers.
- All nonstandard abbreviations and acronyms used in the paper have been defined on first use and used consistently thereafter.
- Abbreviations used in each table have been defined in a note at the bottom of the table.
- The vertical rules/lines have been removed from all three tables.
- The tables are now attached as a separate file instead of embedded in the paper.

I should mention, however, that Table 3 seems a little crowded without the vertical lines separating the information in the columns, and I'm concerned that the presentation may not be as clear as it was with the lines. I see that the guidelines indicate that tables should be on a vertical/portrait page, but I also notice that a few articles in the printed version of the *Journal of Changing Weather* feature tables on a horizontal/ landscape page, so perhaps that would be a good layout for increasing the clarity of Table 3. I'm certainly open to any suggestions you have for this table.

I'm also attaching a certificate from Proof-Reading-Service.com verifying that the article has been professionally proofread with special attention to meeting the *Journal of Changing Weather* author guidelines for formatting, structure and referencing.

I hope that the changes I've made resolve all your concerns about the article. I'm more than happy to make any further changes that will improve the paper and/or facilitate successful publication.

Thank you once again for your time and interest. I look forward to hearing from you.

Sincerely,

[sign here for a formal letter]

Sandra Jones